OCEANIA
NEOCOLONIALISM, NUKES & BONES

OTHER BOOKS FROM ATUANUI PRESS

On Tongan Poetry by ʼI. Futa Helu

Waiheathens: Voices from a Mining Town by Mark Derby,
paintings by Bob Kerr

Toa by Vaughan Rapatahana

OCEANIA
NEOCOLONIALISM, NUKES & BONES

André Vltchek

Foreword by Noam Chomsky
Introduction by Dr Steven Ratuva

Atuanui Press

Published by Atuanui Press Ltd
1416 Kaiaua Road
Pokeno 2473
Auckland, New Zealand

http://atuanuipress.co.nz
editor@atuanuipress.co.nz

CONTENTS

Foreword

André Vltchek has compiled a stunning record in evoking the reality of the contemporary world, not as perceived through the distorting prisms of power and privilege, but as lived by the myriad victims.

He has also not failed to trace the painful—and particularly for the West, shameful—realities to their historical roots.

The remarkable scope of his inquiries is illustrated even by the titles of some of his major books: *Western Terror: From Potosi to Baghdad*, a vast range of topics that he explores with rare insight and understanding; and *Exile*, his interviews with Indonesia's great novelist Pramoedya, who spent a large part of his life in internal exile, imprisoned by the murderous and vicious Suharto government in Indonesia, which was greatly admired by the West, and enthusiastically supported in its shocking crimes, after it won approval by carrying out a mass slaughter that opened up the rich resources of the country to Western exploitation.

In the present work, Vltchek extends his penetrating gaze to a lovely, desecrated, almost forgotten vast area of the world, Oceania, which he shows to be "a microcosm of almost all major problems faced by our planet."

Again, he tears away the scabs and reveals the festering sores below with the insight, acuity, and sympathetic understanding he has shown in his earlier work.

At the same time, once again, he brings to light the strength and courage of the people, and their achievements, and explores the hopes for decent recovery and survival if the powerful can allow themselves to comprehend what they have done, and to accept the responsibility of actually protecting their victims instead of mouthing comforting and self-serving slogans.

—Noam Chomsky

Introduction — THE PERILOUS OCEANIA?

Images of Oceania have graced novels, academic analysis, art canvases, films and increasingly, consultancy reports with often diverse flavour and conclusions. On one extreme of the continuum are those who romanticise the Pacific as the unspoiled Garden of Eden of 'noble savages' in their innocent and atavistic state and on the other extreme end are doomsday prophets who see everything in the Pacific as hellish and destined for eternal damnation. There are shades of perception oscillating between the two depending on the ideological orientation, cultural worldview and mood of the beholder.

This book by André Vltchek can be placed somewhere in between. It is a critical appraisal of the destructive consequences of colonialism and later neocolonialism and how they have reshaped and undermined the very essence of Pacific humanity. It provides a rather uncomfortable but justifiably powerful moral message that the perils of Oceania need drawing attention to for the future survival of Pacific peoples and cultures who, isolated from the main centres of global power, are often relegated to the margins of development and progress.

Underpinning the detailed and vibrant narrative is the belief that post-colonial development has gone horribly wrong because of the way in which former colonies in the Pacific have replicated the inappropriate and patronizing political, economic and cultural institutions and norms of the crisis-prone European civilization. Global imperialism did not come to an end after decolonization but rather reinvented itself into more complex, more sophisticated and more influential ways through investment, trade, education, cultural influence or just naked economic exploitation.

Oceania: neocolonialism, nukes and bones is a panoramic view of some of the smallest states but at the same time, some of the most vibrant cultures in the world. It provides both a broad brush of the Pacific as well as a more microscopic examination of specific problems of specific countries.

Beyond the sympathetic gaze of a foreign journalist, the book also echoes some of the deeply entrenched views and sentiments of the Pacific people who, because of their isolation and 'smallness,' are often ignored in mainstream literature and discourse. Vltchek takes up the same challenge as Fijian-Tongan anthropologist, Prof Epeli Hauofa, whom he praises as "one of the region's leading intellectuals." The challenge is to invert some colonially framed perspectives of the Pacific which have denigrated and distorted Pacific cultures, worldviews and sense of humanity and reframe the world in a more empowering way. In his book *Our Sea of Islands*, Hauofa redefines Oceania's ontology, not in terms of small islands but using the large ocean as the centre of intellectual gravity. This means that the Pacific is actually huge rather than small. In the modern global imagination, size does matter.

It might be easy for some to dismiss Vltchek's book as patronizing and a biblical text of doomsday prophecy but this view misses the point altogether. The underpinning thrust of the book is that the current dynamics in the Pacific in the form of environmental degradation, weak states, militarization, corruption and conflict, are reflective of the way in which external hegemonic forces have reshaped Pacific cultures and institutions to serve, not their own people, but foreign interests.

Although colonialism in its formal manifestation has largely disappeared from Oceania (except for the French colonies of New Caledonia, French Polynesia and Wallis and Futuna) new forms of hegemony pervade in different forms, shapes and sizes. Some like foreign aid are more obvious while some like ideas and values are more subtle and have embedded themselves in Oceanic consciousness in a profoundly transformative way.

The role of foreign consultants and advisors is critical in this new wave of neocolonialism since they provide 'ideas' which shape government policies and recommend projects which impact on the lives of ordinary Pacific people. Vltchek refers to them as the "modern-era conquistadores with a generous salary and a per diem." Armed with laptops and minimal knowledge of the Pacific, many of these bearers of wisdom traverse the islands and use them as living laboratories for their neoliberal ideals.

The Pacific peoples' resistance to external hegemony has been a cornerstone of their political and social transition. Although on the surface, they may appear to be as reserved and innocent as the classical stereotype would suggest, the history of their anti-colonial struggle has been part of the bigger picture of coming to terms with the outside world as they try to protect their sovereignty and redefine their new identity. The anti-colonial Mau movement in Samoa in the early 1900s, the anti-British western Fijian rebellion in the late 1800s, the continuing sovereignty movements in Hawaii and Aotearoa (New Zealand), the independence movement in Vanuatu in the 1960s and 70s, and the continuing anti-colonial movements in the French and American colonies are just some manifestations of these. Rebellion took different forms, some overtly political, some based on cultural resistance and some articulated through psychological symbolism. Today, the fact that there is no violent public opposition of the 'Arab Spring' type does not indicate lack of resistance. There are often complex modes of engagement, and resistance can be contextual and very subtle. In many Pacific cultures, the use of humour is one of the most subtle and most psychologically effective forms of resistance.

The formation of the Nuclear Free and Independent Pacific movement (NFIP) in 1975 was the culmination of regional solidarity in the face of the colonial and neocolonial onslaught. The movement started as a protest group against the French nuclear testing on Moruroa Atoll in French Polynesia and it expanded to become the vanguard of anti-nuclear, pro-independence, human rights, indigenous rights and environmental campaigns in the Pacific. It was the most cohesive and most high profile anti-colonial front in the Pacific which represented the voices of the subdued Pacific peoples.

The vestiges of colonialism have not withered away totally. They have simply been repackaged and resold in more attractive forms. Post-colonial education and localization has led to the creation of a new breed of elites whose taste, economic interests and political ideologies mirror those of the colonial masters. But they can readily leverage the fact that they are locally born, speak the local language and articulate the local cultural views as the legitimizing façade behind which they squander and exploit the poor locals. The examples around the Pacific shown in this book are testimony to this.

Armed with international degrees, gold credit cards and gold frequent flyer status, this cadre of local middle class upstarts have enriched themselves and consolidated their social status and political power by leveraging both modern and traditional means of social mobility.

Vltchek argues that "Oceania is a microcosm of almost all major problems faced by our planet." This makes sense in the context of the way in which the Pacific became tangled up with global problems of power contestation. Oceania became a theatre of war in WWII and a nuclear weapons testing ground for the British (Christmas Island in Kiribati), United States (Bikini Atolls in the Marshall Islands) and French (in Moruroa Atoll, French Polynesia). The Japanese dumped their nuclear waste in the north Pacific and so did the Americans. The Chinese also tested their rocket carriers in the Pacific just like the Americans who have been doing it for years up to the present day. During the cold war, the Pacific was dotted with US military bases to contain possible Soviet expansion and for some time it was referred to as the 'American Lake.' Both powers used the large ocean as a playground for their naval 'chicken game.' A new cold war of sorts is being resurrected with the growth in Chinese interests in Oceania and subsequent US military, political and economic response in the form of the 'pivot' doctrine. This will see further militarization and tension in Oceania.

Renewed US interests in the Pacific in the last 5 years have been due largely to the increase in Chinese influence and fear by the US of its diminished power and prestige in this part of the world. Chinese aid is the most sought after by the Pacific island states because of its focus on infrastructure, compared to Australian aid which is largely invisible with about 80% of the money going back to Australia through its consultants.

The impact of neoliberalism is transforming the economic, social and political face of the small Pacific states in a variety of ways. The free trade negotiations with Australia and New Zealand under the Pacific Agreement on Closer Economic Relations (PACER-plus) has now stalled, and so has the free trade negotiations with the European Union under the Economic Partnership Agreement (EPA). Part of the reason is that the Pacific states are resisting being drawn into free trade agreements from which they will not benefit, and will exacerbate their demise given their lack of products to sell to the bigger trading partners. PACER-plus is being pushed by Australia and New Zealand, the two dominant powers in the Pacific Island Forum.

Oceania: neocolonialism, nukes and bones' insight into some of the troublesome issues in the Pacific brings the Pacific closer to a world audience which often sees the Pacific only as a place of eternal romance and divine beauty where film stars spend their holidays and where life is untouched by the vagaries of modernity. The increasingly perilous life of many Pacific peoples is directly linked to their increasing incorporation into a global system which reinforces stratification based on economic and political power. Being at the bottom of the heap and being able to see the world and change things from that vantage point is always a challenging task particularly in a world where competition based on capacity to dominate is the norm.

The style and intent of this book has the potential to win a wide and informed audience. It is destined to be a journalistic masterpiece, laced with a deep sense of morality and commitment for the betterment of a forgotten part of the world.

—Dr Steven Ratuva

Acknowledgements

I would like to express deep gratitude to all the people of Oceania who shared their stories and opened their hearts during my work in this region.

In particular, thanks to the great writer and my friend Epeli Hau'ofa who offered his full support to this book, even elevating the author to the ranks of 'honorary citizen of Oceania.'

I would also like to thank the great Tongan poet and educator Konai Helu Thaman and the Fijian educator and writer Joseph Veramu who traveled with the author throughout Samoa and the western part of Viti Levu island in Fiji, discussing many of the burning social issues his country is presently facing. I would also like to thank Espen Ronneberg, Climate Change Advisor at the Secretariat of the Pacific Environmental Programme (SPREP)—for his help with the environmental issues and everything connected to the Marshall Islands.

Also, I would also like to thank two brave Senators from Kwajalein Atoll of Marshall Islands (RMI): former foreign minister Tony deBrum and Paramount Chief Michael Kabua, the staff of the newspaper of *Samoa Observer*, *Marshall Island Journal*, *Solomon Star* and *The National* of PNG; the local government at Kwajalein, RMI, and the great educators in Tonga, Kiribati, Fiji, Palau and Cook Islands.

My warm thanks go to the Permanent Secretary of Education of Kiribati—Teekoa Ietaake.

I would like to thank UNESCO, FAO and UNDP staff in Oceania for their help and great discussions, and I would like to express my gratitude to several organizations including Greenpeace, Samoa's Victim Association, Fiji Women's Rights Movement (FWRM), National Disaster Management Office in Tuvalu, and very importantly, to The Center for Environmental Law and Community Rights and its chief lawyer Demien Ase.

I would like to thank Prof. Mark Selden who published many of my articles on Oceania in his highly acclaimed academic magazine *Japan Focus* and who later helped significantly with the editing process. I am very grateful to him for not murdering me in the process.

I would like to thank my proofreader and editor Terry Collins for dedicated and excellent work. I would also like to express gratitude to an Australian cultural expert with great experience in Oceania—Emily Waterman.

My heartfelt thanks go to Noam Chomsky and Michael Parenti for reading my manuscript when it was still in the form of separate articles, commenting and supporting my efforts.

And most importantly, I would like to thank Yayoi Segi— without her help, support and tremendous dedication to Oceania this book would have never seen the light!

— André Vltchek

Preface —
PACIFIC JOURNEY

ALMOST EVERY VOYAGE HAS ITS BEGINNING AND END, but mine seems to have been going in circles for more than five years. I have worked in Oceania as a journalist as well as for international organizations: writing reports, taking photographs, producing books and covering stories ranging from the sinking of entire nations as a result of global warming to the devastating impact of a US military base on a remote Micronesian atoll.

Even in the 21st century, almost no journey through Oceania is easy—international ferry connections are close to non-existent; airplane routes are shrinking, overpriced and often irrational. Time and again, I spent days waiting for an international connection in Fiji or the Solomon Islands and longer still waiting for a domestic link to some remote and sparsely inhabited island group or atoll. And there are still some countries and island groups I—a determined explorer—never managed to visit: Niue, Nauru and Tokelau: a New Zealand colony.

I developed deep feelings of attachment to this universe of flying fish, gentle reflections of the descending sun in turquoise water, stilt houses, impenetrable jungle bordering white sand beaches and fantastic coral rims. But above all I felt increasingly close to the men and women of Oceania with their arsenal of stories, passions, references and ways of life. Here I found emotions and instincts that are often concealed in more populous, prosperous and influential parts of the world. But I didn't come to 'study them' as some anthropologists like Margaret Mead have done; as a writer I came to listen to their stories, attempting to 'translate' them or simply bring them to the rest of the world.

Precisely because of my love for the land, water and people of the islands, my concern for the future grew, I often felt helpless and overwhelmed by the magnitude of the problems they confront.

Yet I never lost faith in the wisdom of the local people and their culture—in their ability to regenerate, to survive and to preserve what they see as worth preserving and defending. But I also knew that for Oceania to survive and to flourish, there has to be regional unity and a total collapse of imaginary walls and borders erected by the colonizers. There has to be one unifying voice defending common goals; one ocean and thousands of islands inhabited by people united in their diversity. Visiting almost all nations and territories I strongly believe that such a scenario is possible and within reach!

I often felt that I had 'seen it all' in Oceania—the beauty and the misery, the cynicism of neocolonial rulers and local elites and the impact of the 'free market' on poor nations and people; but there was always much more to see and even now, temporarily leaving Oceania, I feel that there is still so much more to learn about this unique and diverse part of the world located at the edge of almost all world maps.

Once I decided to write a book that would address the major issues facing Oceania today in light of its historical trajectory, I often had to work from scratch. To exchange ideas, I had to travel thousands of miles, as very little substantial information was available in print or online and people of the islands are reluctant to discuss serious issues over the phone. Eventually I amassed hundreds of pages of notes, hours of interviews on mini discs as well as tens of thousands of images. Documenting the plight of Oceania became a mission.

Oceania is a microcosm of almost all major problems faced by our planet. In all 14 independent nations and in several colonies (mostly called, politely, territories), I witnessed appalling problems. Major and minor regional and global players were ravaging natural resources with disastrous environmental consequences, and had performed nuclear experiments on the islands and the inhabitants of Oceania.

Entire countries inhabited by people with their own distinct culture used for political purposes. Entire nations were forced into dependent relationships with one of the powers, and this forced the often shrinking populations into idleness and hopelessness.

As it has done for decades elsewhere, the international mainstream mass media reacted by simplifying the issues and ignoring the legacy of history: victims of colonialism and neocolonialism were accused of corruption without reference to the historical dynamics that had taken so heavy a toll on the islands and their residents.

Local elites, without exception educated in the USA, Australia, France and New Zealand, and with little understanding of the problems that local people confront, defined how men and women of Oceania are supposed to see themselves, and their position in the world.

Cut off from each other by the trappings of colonialism—borders and other political boundaries—the people of Oceania became isolated from one another. With their culture and way of life under constant threat, I witnessed entire nations in an unmistakable state of deep depression, hopelessness and frustration. In some places, although naturally not everywhere, the old stories had disappeared together with much of the traditional lifestyles. Frustration and loss of self-respect led to obesity, alcoholism, child abuse and other forms of violent behavior. Virulent nationalism, even racism, took root in some islands that had known no borders in the past.

Eventually, I felt it was time to act, to tell the story. But the story was spread across thousands of miles of seemingly endless ocean. I had no funding and no institutional backing. While thousands of 'advisors' and 'international development workers' were receiving hefty monthly fees and per diems for maintaining the status-quo and facilitating the dominance of the regional powers in Oceania, I was spending almost all that I earned elsewhere on travel to and within Oceania, collecting data, interviewing people and recording images depicting their plight. I don't regret this—it was both an honor and a privilege and it allowed me to experience tremendous adventures.

Being on my own I had no handlers and nobody to report to—I was free to choose my own angle and my own stories, beholden only to the people of the islands. My journey of many years through the Pacific has been rewarding.

Oceania is home to some of the most distinctive and wonderful people on earth—both native, and 'implanted' from all over the world. As a novelist and filmmaker I encountered hundreds of unusual stories and stunning images; in sum, new and essential perspectives from which to view life.

I set off to learn as much as I could. And I was sharing my stories from South and North America, Asia, Europe and Africa with those men and women of Oceania who were willing to listen.

I met Epeli Hau'ofa, now deceased, who was probably Oceania's greatest writer.

I met traditional storytellers from the 'headhunter's coast' on the Solomon Islands. I spoke to diverse people such as mercenary officers of the Fijian military, a Tongan poet, an environmental lawyer from Papua New Guinea, the Minister of Foreign Affairs of the Marshall Islands, an educator-priest from the Federated States of Micronesia, a victim of child abuse in Samoa, a shark-feeder from French Polynesia and an artisan on Easter Island. I spoke to hundreds of victims and to some victimizers—to those who hold power and to those who are selling their own countries for luxurious condominiums in Sydney, Honolulu and Auckland.

In writing this book, I have tried to address some of the major problems Oceania presently confronts. While I hope researchers and academia will use this book, it is not a book for academics. Such a work would disqualify many of the people of Oceania and many visitors to the region and general readers as potential readers. For the same reason I decided against the use of footnotes. Agonizing over style, I finally chose plain journalistic language in an attempt to convey the lively thought and language of a range of local people. Above all, I have written this book with readers in Oceania in mind.

In 2008, sitting at a table at the Barrister Cafe on the campus of the University of the South Pacific in Suva, Fiji, I asked Epeli Hau'ofa whether it was too arrogant for me to write a long book on Oceania as a traveler from afar. He stared at me for a while, kindly but ironically. "How many years have you worked in Oceania?" He asked. "Five," I replied. "Do you care about this part of the world?" "A lot," I said. "That qualifies you as one of us," he said. "You are from Oceania. And as such, you can; you are actually obliged to write what is happening here. Especially since most of us can't or don't know how."

Amen!

Taking seriously Epeli's urging, I have attempted to write a book that speaks for the often silent people of the archipelago, that gives voice to their hopes and aspirations as well as their pain and suffering. I have written as one describing a desperate and battered but nevertheless deeply loved home.

The New Pacific Wall:
THE GREAT POWERS ISOLATE AND DIVIDE THE INSULAR NATIONS

L ONG REPORTS HAVE BEEN COMPILED ON THE SUBJECT of the dependency of the Pacific Islands and the financial burdens this places on the United States, Australia, New Zealand and other 'benevolent' and 'charitable' nations. Dozens of conferences and international meetings have addressed the 'ess-ential issues': "Are the people of Oceania too spoiled or too lazy? Are their leaders too corrupt and incapable to govern their countries effectively? If charity dries up, what will become of Oceania?"

Of course, this precise terminology was not used; discussions took place in an orderly fashion, adhering to the norms of political correctness.

Leaders and especially the common people of Oceania were 'shamed and put in their place' in the most polite and refined ways, addressed as 'Sir' and 'Madam'. Our governments humiliated them, as did our media and hundreds of so called international advisors. To summarize who exactly these international advisers are is not difficult: they are modern-era conquistadores with a generous salary and a per diem. A large part of so-called foreign aid budgets goes for their fantastic island-hopping voyages. Their main task is to increase the political, economical and ideological influence of their countries on the region while providing as little tangible assistance as possible.

Oceania, without Australia and New Zealand, is inhabited by fewer than 10 million people, most of them economically poor. Combined, it is in possession of great natural resources from which at the moment it hardly benefits. International—mainly Malaysian—logging companies made off with almost all of the valuable timber of Oceania, deforesting large parts of the Solomon Islands and Papua New Guinea (PNG). Mining companies from across the globe, including Australian, US and Canadian conglomerates, sank their teeth into the veins and guts of both independent and still colonized parts of Oceania, leaving devastated areas in the Solomon Islands, Nauru, New Caledonia, and Fiji, to mention just a few. The Indonesian province of West Papua in particular has been almost irreversibly ruined, culturally, environmentally and socially, by Indonesian colonialism and its foreign corporate associates.

Over-fishing, particularly by the fleets belonging to northeast Asian countries, has reached epic proportions.

The USA., UK and France tested their nuclear weapons in the pristine waters of Micronesia and Polynesia. Several major powers attempted to dump their waste—nuclear and 'conventional'—in the middle of this enormous, and until recently, unspoiled part of the world, while Australia periodically uses Oceania for detention camps housing 'illegal' refugees that have reached or attempted to reach its shores.

Young boys from the Marshall Islands, Samoa, Guam, Tonga and elsewhere go to Iraq, Afghanistan and other war zones seeking glory or at least a wage in response to propaganda campaigns or in financial desperation; many die or are mutilated. And Fijian mercenaries returning from dirty jobs, usually for North American or British employers, in faraway war zones keep staging military coups in their own country. As if the Fijian example were not enough, Australia and New Zealand are presently helping to set-up the army in the tiny kingdom of Tonga, where the US is training soldiers in preparation for 'humanitarian missions' abroad.

Historically, in this part of the world there were no frontiers, just one great ocean both dividing and uniting islands and communities, one ocean to sail and one enormous sky filled with stars to help people of the ocean navigate their vessels. But the last few centuries have brought invasions, conquests and above all division. Borders were drawn along arbitrary lines in the midst of a seemingly free and unconquerable mass of water. Obsessed with wealth and power, conquerors introduced a fascination with material possessions to societies whose cultures were often based on communal ownership and support—a pattern common in so many other colonized parts of the world. The colonialists spread their religion and introduced their laws, so there could be no doubt which rules and which games had to be honored and revered.

The first invaders swindled local people out of their land and their natural resources, often for a few glass trinkets or other trifles, employing the same tactics used earlier in what is now called Latin America. What they didn't manage to take by deception and fraud, they took by brute force inflicting great loss of life.

British, French, US and other Western ships sailed to the shores of many Pacific islands. Women were raped and food and water supplies plundered, and local people were taken away as slaves.

Great lessons of 'civilization' were delivered by 'developed' nations who fought devastating wars against each other in the sea and on the islands and atolls of Oceania, with spite and disregard for the local population. Only the Japanese army bothered to evacuate local civilians from several battlefields, including those in today's Palau.

And when the guns had fallen silent on some of the most horrific battlefields of World War II, western nations set off nuclear tests with devastating effects on the natives and on the environment. They moved some of the people from contaminated islands and studied the medical and social consequences as if they were guinea pigs.

Colonizers then said to the people of Oceania: Be independent, as long as you profess our political system and our 'free market' way of doing business—as long as our companies can do what they want on your isles and your governments vote for the UN resolutions we draw up. Be free and we will help you by sending advisors to build your armies even if there is nobody you want to fight right now. Be free as long as you send your boys to our battalions, and as long as you keep at bay those we don't like, such as the Chinese and Russians. What's more, we will train your leaders in our schools so they understand how important it is to treasure private property and long for profit. In exchange, we will give you our frozen food and sugary sodas so you can taste how sweet civilized life can be.

When the exhausted, robbed and restless people of Oceania sat in confusion on their shores, staring at their dear old friends—the stars, the endless ocean—in expectation of the answers, thinking what to do next; anthropologists, international experts and advisers from Sydney, Auckland, Los Angeles and who knows where else, became concerned. "They are lazy and too fat,", they whispered. "They never had to work. They expect the rest of the world to feed them. But what can we do? We are good people and we won't let them starve. We can't just watch these simple men and women go hungry and bankrupt."

"New Zealand may claim that its aid to a particular small country is far in excess of any economic benefit it gains in return. But New Zealand's overall trade with the Pacific Islands as a whole is so much in its favor that its total aid outlay goes only a modest way towards correcting the imbalance," explained one of the most accomplished thinkers of Oceania, Tongan writer Epeli Hau'ofa.

"The same is true of Australia, except that much of its monetary aid never leaves the country or it may leave like a tourist only to fly back home in great comfort and loaded with duty-free goods." The point is that when the flows of resources within the region are added up, Australia and New Zealand come up well ahead. For what they give out in aid they receive in return a great deal more in the forms of export earnings and repatriation of profits on investments. It may be said that as far as the regional relationships and resource flows are concerned, if the words 'aid' and 'help' are to be used at all, they should more correctly be used in terms of the small islands 'aiding' their two big neighbors and others such as the United States.

Concealed aid keeps flowing from these tiny islands to the mighty corporate headquarters and capitals all over the world. It is not as much as what is escaping from much larger nations in South America, Africa and Asia, but for corporate leaders and for the governments sponsored by corporations, every penny counts. By now, the islands of Oceania have lost many of their resources. They have also lost millions of their people—often the most talented and enterprising—who abandoned the islands searching for a better life abroad or for better ways to support their impoverished families back home. Paradoxically, they often sail to the shores inhabited by those who deprived their islands of their future.

Chances for the islands of Oceania to become rich members of the world community decreased dramatically—coming close to zero—as collective bargaining was dismissed by their corrupt leaders (trained and educated abroad, as promised) who chose personal enrichment over the unity and strength of the island peoples. And as the islands and their people grow weaker, the outsiders are dividing and ruling, doing what they know best—building a tall and sturdy Pacific wall with very few gates, to which they alone hold the keys.

The once free, proud and adventurous people of the ocean: Pacific Islanders—have become imprisoned in ridiculous Western concepts called nation-states, ruled by corrupt leaders almost exclusively educated and trained in metropolises of the invading states.

AN IMAGINARY ELECTRONIC FENCE WITH
WATCHTOWERS IN THE MIDDLE OF THE OCEAN

It is said that colonialism in Oceania (involving France, the UK, the US, Spain, Germany, Japan, Australia, and New Zealand), was less brutal than in some other parts of the world. Apart from Rapa Nui, there was no island group where almost the entire population was exterminated, as happened in the Caribbean and elsewhere, although people of several atolls lost their homes due to nuclear experiments and continue to lose out due to global warming. Nevertheless, the boundaries that were erected in the colonial and post-colonial periods have destroyed traditional ways of life.

As a result of colonialism and neocolonialism, most of the newly independent nations were unaccustomed to standing on their own feet, instead accepting their fate as de facto dependencies of their former colonial masters or other powers. Expressions of their culture and beliefs, discouraged, even at times banned, simply disappeared.

Polynesia, Melanesia and Micronesia span a tremendous area of the planet but are inhabited by only a handful of people, fewer than 10 million in total. 'Supporting' them proved to be dirt-cheap for the new masters of the Pacific—the United States, Australia, New Zealand and France. Having client states at their disposal yields great returns.

The United States negotiated a so-called 'Compact of Free Association' (COFA) with three officially independent states in Micronesia (former de facto colonies)—the Federated States of Micronesia (FSM), the Republic of the Marshall Islands (RMI) and the Republic of Palau. In exchange for cold cash and the right for Micronesians to live and study in the United States, all three countries, after some arm twisting and financial persuasion, agreed to host US military bases on their territories. So far the bases have been built only on RMI, but this could change at anytime.

"For the US, the most important factor behind the Compact was a so-called 'strategic denial' for Soviet ships," explains Francis X. Hezel, a leading scholar on Micronesia and head of the Micronesian Seminar. "FSM covers an enormous ocean area and by signing the Compact, the entire territory became a no-go area for ships from those countries that the US considers hostile to its interests. Ironically, the Compact was implemented just a few years before the end of the Cold War."

In the library of the Micronesian Seminar are several declassified US State Department documents which clearly state that Japan exercised much more socially conscious and humane control over Micronesia than the US did after World War Two.

Citizens of all three Compact countries went through rigorous Cold War-style indoctrination in classrooms and through the media.

Isaac Soaladaob, former director of the Bureau of Foreign Affairs of Palau and one of the negotiators of the Compact, barely hides his bitterness:

> As you are aware, we were colonized by Spain, Germany, Japan, and the United States. Declassified documents we can now access clearly show that the US was out to Americanize the entire Micronesia. They wanted to change our culture. Before the Japanese occupation, there was no concept of private property or ownership; we had our own traditional societies that were based on collectivism. But that type of society

was not conducive to the capitalist system that the US wanted to implement. We were fooled so many times … we wanted to be nuclear-free, because we knew that the Enola Gay left for Hiroshima from this part of the world, from Saipan.

We also saw the devastation to the Marshall Islands—we saw what happened to our Micronesian brothers—where nuclear tests had been carried out. But we negotiated with the US—it was during the Cold War, after all—and we were told that "We have to be protected." People here were indoctrinated. Of course, there was not one communist around here and people had no idea what was happening in Russia, but they were petrified of communists. In those days we had almost no visitors from abroad and we were not allowed to travel. In the early 1950s we could only travel to the United States.

We never realized that in truth our traditional culture was much closer to communism than to capitalism … we were colonized and thoroughly brainwashed. Then you know what happened during the vote; all that arm-twisting … I know because I was the chair of the constitutional amendment. And now, after all that, this government considers the US, Japan, Australia, and Taiwan to be our best friends: in that order. We even have our men serving in Afghanistan now, and in Iraq. Our people are easily fooled. They learned that it is easiest to be associated with the strongest. They are even proud of their position … oh, and you know, Bush said he is grateful to Palau.

Palau could easily be designated as a case study of how the

Compact (COFA) came to life. As mentioned, there was a lot of US arm-twisting. Eight heated referenda each failed to obtain the 75 percent approval required to over-ride the Constitution's anti-nuclear provision. Finally, the pro-Compact government amended the Palau Constitution, allowing the treaty to be ratified by a simple majority vote. The essence of the Compact is that in exchange for a large cash infusion, Palau gives the US unlimited rights to build military bases. The Palau Constitution is anti-nuclear and it is known that large US military ships are either nuclear-powered, carry nuclear weapons, or both. The US refused to give any assurances that its ships would be nuclear-free and the government of Palau finally opted for a 'don't ask, don't tell' policy.No military base has yet been built in Palau, but the prospect of future bases makes many citizens of this idyllic archipelago profoundly uncomfortable.

With a tiny population of around twenty thousand, Palau forms a long archipelago, which spreads across an enormous mass of water close to the neighboring Philippines and the Indonesian territory of West Papua—two large insular Southeast Asian countries torn by civil conflicts and wars. The US calls the military conflict in Mindanao, in which it is illegally—in breach of the Philippines' constitution—involved, a 'second front in the War Against Terrorism.'

Indonesia, with the largest Muslim population in the world, faces massive social problems and potential instability. It is also one of the richest countries on earth in terms of natural resources, many explored by international mining, oil and logging companies as a result of deals signed by former dictator, US ally Suharto and multi-national conglomerates.

There can be no doubt that the $500 million that the US has spent so far on Palau through COFA and a total of $3.5

billion in funding for 20 years for both FSM and RMI—the Compact was renewed in 2003—has been an extremely 'good deal' for the empire which thus gained control over part of the largest ocean expanses anywhere in the world, inhabited by a defenseless population spread thinly around the island groups. Each nation can potentially host offensive military bases against Asian targets, including China.

Palau, FSM and RMI are located astride essential international maritime shipping routes and therefore cover significant parts of the Pacific, but they are not serving as welcoming transit points for travelers that one would expect given the nature of their culture. Instead, they are part of the fence—the wall. Their role is to 'exclude' and 'deter'. And if the empire asks, and gives a payment in advance, they are obliged to surrender territory to the US military. No questions asked. No exceptions allowed. Palau, FSM and RMI have no right to choose allies in a potential war. They have to line up behind Washington's banner, whatever the conflict and whatever the state of international opinion.

To illustrate how good a deal this is for Washington: the Nimitz-class aircraft carrier cost the US taxpayers approximately $4.5 billion. FSM and RMI, two 'independent' countries, combined are a real bargain: $1 billion less, and for 20 years!

In his monumental encyclopedic study *The South Pacific*, Ron Crocombe argues that US interests in the region have been mainly military, and mainly north of the equator:

> By the Monroe Doctrine, the USA arrogates to itself a controlling interest down the whole Pacific coast of North and South America. That interest spread throughout the Pacific Basin.

US policy was explained in 1981 by Noel Koch, head of International Security in the US Department of Defense. He noted that the 9,400 US military personnel in Guam and Micronesia "underscores our intention of preserving US interests [and] ... achieving a position of consequence in the Pacific Island states." American Samoa provided the USA with "a potential point for power projection in the South Pacific ... [as USA Pacific territories were] inextricably linked to overall USA foreign policy and economic interests." To maximize US interests they needed 'close and friendly relations' with Pacific people and governments, so his department had a 'strong and continuing interest' in the success of other [American] agencies.

These initiatives were described at the same time by Assistant Secretary of State John Holdridge, who said that, to advance its interests, the USA was increasing aid and diplomatic representation, offering influential Islanders trips to the USA "which has had a very positive impact," supporting regional cooperation, coordinating with Australia and New Zealand, resolving territorial claims, using the Peace Corps, becoming more involved in communications, and sending more warships on goodwill visits ....

As Pacific nations became independent, the USA became more involved. In 1976 it supplied Fiji, at a token price, with ships to establish a small navy. In the 1980s it supplied US military training and liaison personnel, and equipment. A former military aid program, begun in 1985, was later expanded to PNG and Tonga. In 1978-79, in return for finally relinquishing spurious claims to much of the Cook Islands, Kiribati and Tuvalu, those countries were persuaded to sign treaties giving the USA strategic leverage.

There was also, of course, the great plan, discussed earlier, called Compact of COFA on the part of the US, which brought under full political and military control all three countries of Micronesia: Palau, Federated States of Micronesia (FSM) and Republic of Marshall Islands (RMI). Ron Crocombe further argues:

> It was cheaper, easier and more acceptable to the USA to influence the Islands indirectly, in a modern equivalent of the British colonial policy of 'indirect rule'. Some functions were 'sub-contracted' to Australia and, to a lesser extent, New Zealand. The USA was also one of many foreign powers to use Fiji as a pivotal state through which to lever other Pacific countries. The US government worked directly and through surrogates such as the Asia Foundation, to maximize influence over Pacific media and governments....

In 2007, with Australian and New Zealand prompting—due to their fear of China—and the US government's dawning realization that it had lost influence in the region, the USA introduced new and expanded programs of aid, familiarization visits for leaders, propaganda inputs to media, visits by US speakers to the region, education programs, Peace Corps workers, grants to NGOs and the standard international range of soft fronts to back up military, coast guard and other more directly strategic actions.

Oceania is not only providing bases for the US military and 'strategic denial' against its foes, real and potential. It supplies the flesh—literally the cannon fodder—of Polynesian, Melanesian and Micronesian boys who are consistently recruited by the US military. They are fighting and dying in conflicts to impose the New World Order in faraway lands. They do it for cash, but some also do it for glory—having been taught that it is honorable to live and die under the banner of freedom and democracy. They heard it on the radio and saw it on TV. The media in Oceania is fully dependent on outside 'help'—through the free releases from foreign press agencies to seminars that teach locals how to be 'good journalists'. Those who control their islands, advising them how to live and think and how to interpret the world, have never allowed alternative views to penetrate the psyche of the islanders. And the wall is high, making it hard to hear and comprehend what is said on the other side.

FOREIGN POLICY MAKERS AND ALLIANCES ... IN WHOSE INTERESTS?

Conditions for an autonomous foreign policy for the small Pacific countries are almost non-existent. Some independent countries, like Nauru, are hopelessly bankrupt; other countries—Tuvalu, Kiribati and the Marshall Islands—are 'sinking' as a result of global climate change. There are low-key civil conflicts and wars battering PNG and the Solomon Islands and what Western experts like to call 'dependency syndrome' is rampant all over Oceania. Almost all nations of the region are experiencing health emergencies due to drastically changed diets and lifestyles. Not one of the 14 'independent' countries is really in a position to negotiate with the rest of the world. All are readily maneuvered into unfavorable arrangements that give large players in the region full control over their domestic and international policy, as well as their economy.

This means that the USA, Australia, EU and New Zealand can always count on obedient and friendly votes on the UN floor, on military recruitment to fight distant wars and conflicts, and on easy access to the natural resources for the companies of the main regional players.

The 14 independent nations, as well as the remaining Pacific colonies, stay hopelessly divided. There is almost no comprehensive attempt at integration that would make it possible to speak with a single voice. Rather several regional organizations provide the appearance of a body that represents the interests of the small countries of Oceania. The most significant of them is the Pacific Island Forum (PIF), but it is dominated by Australia and New Zealand— the two countries that are the biggest 'financial donors' and therefore de facto decision makers. At its annual Leaders Meeting held in Niue in 2008, Australia and New Zealand forced the resignation of Solomon Islander Peter Finau as Deputy Secretary General in favor of a candidate preferred by Australia and New Zealand. The result is that financial, business, trade and political arrangements in the region are dominated by the three major players in Oceania—the US, Australia, and New Zealand—which control the foreign policy and trade of their tiny and vulnerable client-states.

"One day I had an entire television crew from Israel parked at my office," remembers Francis X. Hezel. "I had no idea what they were doing here. Why would they travel so far, to such a small and insignificant country? Finally I understood: the Israeli public was fascinated with this place; they wanted to know 'who are those people who keep voting in the U.N. against Security Council resolutions, in this way supporting Israel and the United States against the entire world ....'

Pacific Island votes at the UN are openly for sale, especially when peace in the Middle East is at stake. To illustrate the absurdity of the game: at a time when several countries in the region are becoming uninhabitable as a result of global warming both Nauru and Kiribati (itself one of the 'sinking nations' and therefore a victim) voted against the Kyoto Protocol.

But it is not only profit that propels tiny nations in Oceania to 'sell their votes' it is also the fear of retribution. "In the late 90s our government voted at the UN against the US on the issue of landmines," recalled the then Foreign Minister of Marshall Islands (RMI) Tony deBrum. "As a result, our party lost the elections."

On October 30th, 2009, *The International Herald Tribune* reported: 'The general Assembly voted overwhelmingly on Wednesday to condemn the US trade embargo against Cuba, with the speeches by the US ambassador and Cuba's foreign minister reflecting what little has changed despite an expected shift under the administration of President Barack Obama.'

The nonbinding resolution has become an annual ritual for 18 years, with a tally this time of 187 in support, 3 opposed and 2 abstaining. The vote underlined the utter lack of support for the 50-year-old American attempt to isolate Cuba. (Israel and Palau joined the United States, while the Marshall Islands and Micronesia abstained.)

Several tiny island nations have found it lucrative to play the Taiwanese card. Quoting local government jargon, Pacific Island nations 'go either with Taiwan or the People's Republic of China.' Palau, for instance, recognizes Taiwan, which calls itself the Republic of China. This translates into investment, aid, and an air link that brings a regular flow of tourists from Taipei.

"Taiwan sees diplomatic recognition by Pacific Island states as an important political weapon in its difficult relationship with China," explains Stuart Harris, a leading specialist in Chinese foreign policy at Australian National University. But Taiwan is not alone.

China similarly seeks to persuade states recognizing Taiwan to change their diplomatic recognition to the People's Republic of China (PRC). It does not cost a lot financially to persuade government leaders in many of these states to see the advantage of changing their state's recognition from China to Taiwan and vice versa.

"The impact of the competition between Taiwan and China," Harris continues, "usually in the form of financial aid, undermines the considerable efforts made in a number of these states, such as the Solomon Islands and in Nauru, to improve regional governance."

The Pacific Island Forum has an official relationship with China, yet six of its 14 members officially recognize Taiwan. At present, Samoa, the Kingdom of Tonga, Cook Islands, Niue, Fiji, Vanuatu, FSM, and PNG 'go with China,' together with two regional powers, Australia and New Zealand, while Palau, the Marshall Islands (RMI), Kiribati, the Solomon Islands, Nauru, and Tuvalu 'are with Taiwan.' Several Pacific Island 'swing' nations switch sides to maximize profits. Everything is out in the open. After 'switching from China to Taiwan,' according to government sources, Mr. Anote Tong, president of Kiribati, responded to vocal critics with disarming honesty: "Well, what can we do? We need to work with the nation that can support us!"

While China had undertaken some large construction

projects in Oceania, Taiwan tends to favor direct cash rewards, including overseas trips, to woo undecided government officials in the Pacific. Taiwanese government officials have been accused of bribing political leaders in Solomon Islands, Kiribati and the Marshall Islands.

Anger erupted in the Solomon Islands in April 2006, when Chinese residents, permanent and temporary, and migrant workers became the main target of protest riots triggered by rumors that Taiwan had paid for the election of the unpopular Snyder Rini as prime minister. Not distinguishing between the Chinese from Taiwan and mainland China, the crowd screamed 'waku,' which is a derogatory word for Asian or Chinese. The Chinatown in the capital of Honiara was almost entirely destroyed by looters and arsonists.

It is obvious that PRC's role in the region is much more positive than that of Taiwan, something that gets lost in media coverage, mainly because the flow of information is largely controlled by the US, Australia and New Zealand. Ron Crocombe writes in his *The South Pacific*:

> China has welcomed many Pacific leaders on official visits and has sent high-level delegations to the South Pacific. It has encouraged cultural ties and established an effective aid program. Of all countries in the world, China is the one whose importance to Oceania is likely to expand most.

Other countries, including Japan, have been known to receive votes on the ground of international organizations in exchange for substantial foreign aid. A Palau government official who did not want to be identified bitterly complained about the embarrassment he felt when his President delivered an undiplomatic speech at the United Nations, advancing Japan's bid for permanent membership on the Security Council. Japan has also been accused of buying support for its whaling activities from the Solomon Islands.

The United States, Australia and New Zealand, all lavish aid donors to the tiny Pacific countries, on a per capita basis but not in real terms, expect compliance from their client states on issues ranging from foreign policy to economy and migration. After decades of one-sided information and media indoctrination, psychologically, the majority of inhabitants of Oceania are convinced that their islands simply cannot do otherwise. They have no chance of surviving without the foreign assistance and foreign control over their politics, economy and development. What is certain is that the elites in these countries have profited enormously while national interests have repeatedly been sacrificed.

Teaching Oceania About Freedom of Movement

It is late at night and the coastal road between Apia, the capital of Samoa, and Faleolo International Airport is busy with traffic. Tonight is a big night: a Boeing 767-300 of Air New Zealand will arrive from Los Angeles and make a brief stop in Samoa before continuing to Tonga and Auckland. This weekly flight is a lifeline for the tiny nation of 180,000 people, separated from the rest of the world by thousands of miles of ocean in all directions.

The closest real supermarket is almost 2 hours flight away in Suva, but there is no direct flight to the Fijian capital from Samoa. Auckland in New Zealand, almost 4 hours away by plane, is the most important Samoan 'city' with a much larger Samoan population than Apia, the capital. Air New Zealand, which flies between Auckland and Samoa five times a week and between Samoa and Los Angeles once a week, takes Samoan immigrants to New Zealand, reunites families, transports gravely ill people to the hospitals, shuttles government officials on their constant trips to foreign destinations, and brings food, medicine, equipment, spare parts and perishable goods into the country.

While control over foreign policy of the Pacific nations is taken for granted, the US, Australia, and New Zealand also have almost unlimited control over who is on the move and who encounters whom throughout Oceania. Freedom of movement was and still is one of the basic pillars of Oceanic culture, but it is disappearing as a result of draconian regulations introduced by 'free and democratic western nations'.

Foreign—US, Australian and New Zealand—immigration and customs officers interrogate at will passengers about the purpose of their journeys, check their luggage, and deny transit. That is because almost all airlines still operating in this vast and sparsely populated region are either major carriers from the US, Australia or New Zealand—Continental Micronesia, Qantas, Air New Zealand—or, as in the case of Fijian national carrier Air Pacific, partially owned by conglomerates from these 'Big 3 countries' (Qantas has large stakes in Air Pacific and Air Niugini. Even the lone 737-800 of Samoan Polynesian Blue is part of the Australian Virgin Blue).

Only one flight a week now connects the two neighboring countries of Samoa and Tonga, and it is the above-mentioned Air New Zealand flight between Los Angeles and Auckland with two intermediary stops.

If Samoan or Tongan citizens wish to visit Papua New Guinea (PNG), they have to fly to Australia and then to Port Moresby from Brisbane or Cairns. The alternative route via Nadi in Fiji is infrequent, arduous and even more expensive. Due to the scarcity of flights, passengers often have to travel through both Auckland and Brisbane. In order to do that, they must obtain an Australian transit visa if the transit time is more than eight hours. But even this eight hour transit visa waiver is rarely respected: according to numerous personal testimonies, airlines often deny boarding to Australian transit points to people from the Pacific Island countries and other developing countries who lack Australian transit visas. To visit any of the countries in Micronesia requires a US transit visa to change planes in Hawaii or Guam and there are no exceptions and no way around it.

The small US embassy in Apia, Samoa, is not authorized to issue visas. Prior to 2008, a Samoan citizen had to first apply for a New Zealand visa, which is not easy to obtain, then pay around $500 for tickets to New Zealand in order to apply for a US transit visa, then wait for the interview, pay a non-refundable deposit and wait again for the highly unlikely positive outcome in order to travel to one of the Micronesian countries. Since 2008, Samoan citizens have been able to submit their visa applications to the US Embassy in Apia. A team of visa officers from the US Embassy in Wellington, New Zealand, travels to Samoa every three to four months and conducts personal interviews for pre-selected applicants.

It is now next to impossible for Fijian citizens to obtain Australian or New Zealand visas, although the great majority had nothing to do with the latest military coup in their country. Punishing Fijian citizens is particularly ludicrous given the fact that the Fijian military was set up because of Western interests after the Second World War. While ordinary people are denied transit in Australia and New Zealand because of the coup, members of the Fijian military, many of them retired, continue to serve as mercenaries and private contractors for the US and UK military, and contractors in both Iraq and Afghanistan.

Both Australia and New Zealand are now adopting the US approach to transit passengers. Countless travelers have accused New Zealand of profiting from visa regulations. Many immigration officers at the US, Australian, and New Zealand gateways are tough, uncompromising and by standards of Oceanic culture, thoroughly arrogant and rude. Not long ago, the prime minister of Papua New Guinea on a regular flight during an official visit to Australia was forced to take off his shoes at the Brisbane airport, triggering a diplomatic stand off between the two neighboring countries.

While ordinary citizens find it extremely difficult to get US, Australian, and New Zealand transit visas to visit neighboring countries, even government officials, diplomats, and UN officials encounter discrimination and harassment. In July 2005, the newly appointed head of UNESCO in the Pacific, Visesio Pongi, was asked to accompany the Director General of UNESCO, Koichiro Matsuura, on an official visit to Palau, the Federated States of Micronesia (FSM), and the Marshall Islands.

To reach Palau, Dr. Pongi, who was traveling on a Tongan passport, had to travel from Samoa to Brisbane, then to Cairns and Guam before arriving in Palau. At Cairns, he was denied a boarding pass because he did not hold a US transit visa. Eventually he was re-routed via Tokyo, as Japan does not require a transit visa to change planes. But in Tokyo he was again prevented from boarding his flight to Palau via

Guam, since changing planes in Guam required a US visa. He argued to no avail that as a high-ranking UN diplomat, he was required to accompany the Director General of UNESCO. He was finally loaded on the last flight from Tokyo to Sydney and from there, humiliated, he traveled back to Samoa via Fiji.

Other officials in the Pacific have similar stories. Shaukat Hakim, a Pakistani administrator of the UNESCO office in Apia, recalls: "Once I had to fly from Dubai to Apia via Singapore and Auckland, but was denied boarding as my plane was supposed to make a short stop in Sydney and I didn't have an Australian transit visa. Before, holders of U.N. diplomatic passports (Laissez Passer) were not required to apply for transit visas in Australia and New Zealand, but lately, everything has become more difficult."

Mali Voi, a former UNESCO cultural expert in Apia, holds a PNG passport, as well as a UN diplomatic passport. Mr. Voi recalls flying to Paris Headquarters via Los Angeles in 1999. "In LA they checked my luggage, despite the fact that I was just transiting. I had to take my shoes off. At one point I felt very scared. They thought that I was Ethiopian. They didn't care that I had a UN passport; they treated me badly. Since then I fly to Paris through Asia."

"Everything changed after 9-11," Mr. Voi continued, "but I don't think it is about security, it is about control. Australia and New Zealand changed their regulations dramatically so that now one needs transit visas to enter the Pacific territories. It makes networking in this part of the world very difficult and that's probably their goal."

"Many people, although not all, in the Pacific still feel allegiance to the US," concluded Mr. Voi. "In some parts we saw Americans as liberators. But that's changing. They have definitely lost my vote. And Australia and New Zealand are playing into US hands. I see it as a new form of colonialism … Australia, for instance, is trying to reaffirm its position in the Pacific. I see this triangle—the US, Australia, and New Zealand—as a main stumbling block for the rest of the countries in this part of the world."

Travel regulations are just one of the problems that citizens of the Pacific nations have to face, but it is a serious one, amounting to something that can easily be described as a New Pacific Wall. The US, Australia, and New Zealand are effectively isolating small and poor countries of Oceania from each other, as well as from the rest of the world. This policy was consolidated and solidified during the Bush-Howard alliance, but even with Labor governing Australia and Obama as president, there is little evidence that the 'wall' is going to come down anytime soon.

In his ground-breaking book *We Are The Ocean*, Epeli Hau'ofa offers a passionate ode on the essential unity and greatness of this part of the world:

> There is a world of difference between viewing the Pacific as 'islands in a far sea' and as 'a sea of islands'. The first emphasizes dry surfaces in a vast ocean far from the centers of power. Focusing in this way stresses the smallness and remoteness of the islands. The second is a more holistic perspective in which things are seen in the totality of their relationships …. Continental men, namely Europeans, on entering the Pacific after crossing huge expanses of ocean, introduced the view of 'islands in a far sea'. From this perspective the islands are tiny, isolated dots in a vast ocean. Later on, continental men—Europeans and American— drew

imaginary lines across the sea, making the colonial boundaries that confined ocean peoples to tiny spaces for the first time. These boundaries today define the island states and territories of the Pacific. I have just used the term 'ocean people' because our ancestors, who had lived in the Pacific for over two thousand years, viewed their world as 'a sea of islands 'rather than 'islands in the sea' ... Theirs was a large world in which peoples and cultures moved and mingled, unhindered by boundaries of the kind erected much later by imperial powers. From one island to another they sailed to trade and to marry, thereby expanding social networks for greater flows of wealth. They traveled to visit relatives in a wide variety of natural and cultural surroundings, to quench their thirst for adventure, and even to fight and dominate ...

Today the world of the people of Oceania is tiny and fragmented. Symbolically, the country called Niue with 1,444 inhabitants (2008 census), is the world's smallest population. After Polynesian Airlines, a Samoan carrier, that used to fly there from Faleaolo, collapsed, the only connection with the rest of the world that Niue can count on is a once-a-week Air New Zealand flight.

Instead of visiting each other's islands, people from this part of the world have to travel to much larger lands, far beyond the horizon, in order to find work, to survive and sustain their families, to educate their children and to treat the sick. Apart from sporadic government visits and sport and cultural exchanges, there seems to be hardly any tourism or trade between the countries of Polynesia, Melanesia and Micronesia.

The people of Oceania believe, and there is significant scientific evidence to support their claims, that their culture comes from Asia. Polynesians, particularly Samoans, claim that their predecessors migrated from Southeast Asia, from what are now Indonesian islands. Scientific theories also point out that Micronesians have roots in indigenous cultures in Taiwan. But it will not be easy for people of Southeast Asia and Oceania to renew long lost ties. Immigration control and regulations at big transit airports—Guam, Honolulu, Auckland, Brisbane, Melbourne, Sydney, Cairns, Darwin and Perth—are as effective a deterrence as watch towers and barbed wire at Cold War borders. They also prevent inhabitants of Southeast Asia and Oceania from having normal and beneficial neighborly relations. Now only a select few can leave and return.

Moreover, US, Australian and New Zealand visa regulations effectively destroy many of the most logical routes between Southeast Asia and South America—those that lead through Oceania. Indonesian citizens don't need a visa to go to Peru or Chile, but in order to catch the LAN (Chile) flight from Sydney via Auckland to Santiago de Chile, they need a New Zealand transit visa even if they do not plan to leave the airport. For a Philippine citizen to travel to neighboring Federated States of Micronesia (FSM) requires a US transit visa, something almost impossible to get except for a handful of local elites.

Samoa, divided between so-called American Samoa, the US territory, and the Independent State of Samoa, previously known as Western Samoa, can't count on a free flow of people between its isles anymore. Recent regulations require citizens of Samoa to apply for special permits to enter the US territory of American Samoa. Samoa retaliated and the two countries inhabited by a single people are now further from reunion than at any other time in their long history.

The situation gets even more Kafkaesque. Citizens of the Federated States of Micronesia (FSM) who wish to travel from the island of Yap to their own capital city, on the island of Pohnpei, have no choice but to fly Continental Micronesia, a US carrier, which makes a stop in Guam. Consequently, people of FSM have to go through US immigration and customs where they are questioned and risk refusal to travel within their own territory. Continental Micronesia is the sole carrier between FSM, Palau, and the Marshall Islands, except for short periods when the national airline of the Marshalls with its 2 propeller planes manages to emerge from bankruptcy and offer infrequent flights.

Except for some relatively short transfers—Samoa to American Samoa and Samoa to Tokelau (still a New Zealand territory but which may soon become independent)—there are almost no scheduled sea links between the countries in Oceania. Cruise ships refuse to take regular passengers and so do most of the cargo vessels. Distances are enormous—the Samoa to Tokelau round-trip sail takes up to nine days of arduous journey—and the fleets of independent nations of Oceania are inadequate and in a state of disrepair, hardly capable of servicing their own outer islands.

Local airlines in the region are going under one after another, as was recently the case with the national carrier of Palau and Polynesian Airlines of Samoa. For years, Polynesian Airlines was in the red, at one point losing its only jet and eventually giving up even its regional Dash-8 aircraft. At the end it was reduced to just a few inter-island routes operated by tiny propeller planes, mainly Twin Otters. Eventually, a new airline 'Polynesian Blue' was formed—a joint venture of Australian budget carrier Virgin Blue (49%), the Samoan government (49%) and Apia hotelier, Aggie Gray (2%). The Boeing 737-800 that used to carry the Polynesian Airlines logo was repainted. Most significantly, while Polynesian Airlines once served its own domestic airstrips on the island of Savaii, the tiny nation of Niue, the Vavau island group in Tonga and several airports in American Samoa, Polynesian Blue now only flies a 737-800 five times a week to Auckland and 3 times a week to Sydney, an almost 6 hour flight—routes that predominantly serve the tourist industry.

Once airlines like Air New Zealand achieve near mo-nopoly in certain parts of Oceania, they mind only their profitability while disregarding the interests of people in the region. Air New Zealand continuously threatens to cut the stopover that is vital for Rarotonga on some flights between Auckland and Los Angeles, literally forcing the government of the Cook Islands, a former New Zealand colony, to come up with state funds to subsidize stopovers that bring tourists from the United States. In 2008, Air New Zealand threat-ened to cut the weekly flight linking Tonga, Samoa and the United States, prompting the Samoan government to start negotiations with both Air Pacific and Hawaiian Airlines about alternatives connecting Samoa with the United States.

Air Nauru collapsed several years ago. Its successor, the Taiwan financed 'Our Airline,' became the only direct carrier between Micronesia and Melanesia, but it periodically halts services and drastically reduces routes. Several regional carriers, including Air Niugini, are partially owned by Australian carrier Qantas, operating routes that profit by almost exclusively bringing tourists and foreign experts to Pacific countries.

The only large full-service airline in Oceania is Fiji-based

Air Pacific, with direct flights to the US and Japan and an extensive regional network. Their equipment includes wide-body Boeing 747-400 and 767-300 jets, as well as a variety of smaller jets and propeller airplanes. Air Pacific serves several Pacific destinations from its Nadi hub, including Kiribati, Samoa, the Kingdom of Tonga, and Vanuatu. Prices are often exorbitant and connecting times inconvenient, but there is no alternative.

The original idea behind Air Pacific was to create a strong regional carrier that would serve both profitable international routes and isolated communities of the Pacific. It was supposed to combine profitability and community service for all Oceania. The airline was profitable until 2005 but it then abandoned its original social commitment, becoming a fully commercial venture which cut almost all regional services except for a profitable route to Papua New Guinea via the Solomon Islands and to the countries—Kiribati, Nauru, Tonga and Samoa—whose governments still held minor stakes in the airline.

While the Fijian government holds a majority stake (51%) in Air Pacific, the largest Australian carrier—Qantas—controls over 46%. It is no longer a force for Pacific integration. Business-oriented in the extreme, it also faces severe financial problems and acute shortages of pilots.

Hundreds of passengers were stranded in the tiny country of Tuvalu in August 2008 due to operational problems of Air Pacific, the only carrier that now connects it with the rest of the world, having replaced Air Fiji that used to fly leased 1950s Convair propeller airplanes to Funafuti Atoll.

In the meantime, Kiribati, which is in terms of geographical size one of the largest countries on earth (its atolls spread across fantastic distances) lost its only international connection to

Christmas Island, a prime tourist site at its Eastern extreme, while even the most populated Tarawa Atoll is served only by a few Boeing 737-700 flights a week, operated by Air Pacific from Nadi.

"We are forced to pay some of the highest prices on earth for terrible service," complained one passenger on a flight bound for Tarawa. "It was not supposed to be like this. Air Pacific was launched as a Pacific airline serving the people of Oceania. But now it is all about business."

On the same flight, an Australian engineer was bound for Tarawa to fit a propeller engine on one of the short-haul aircraft of comatose Air Kiribati. "They didn't fly for weeks," he explained. "It created great problems for the outlying atolls."

THE DEMISE OF A PACIFIC COMMUNITY

Ties to the US, Australia, and New Zealand are replacing Inter-Pacific cultural and economic bonds. The average citizen of Samoa knows much more about life in Auckland than about life in Kiribati, Papua New Guinea or Fiji. People living in Palau are fluent in cultural nuances and attuned to educational opportunities in the United States, while Melanesia and Polynesia are for them just remote and sparsely inhabited areas of the South Pacific.

On the inter-governmental level, there is still a certain will to pursue integration of the region, the most significant attempt being the Pacific Plan approved by the leaders of the Pacific Island countries in Papua New Guinea in October 2005. However, most governments are weak and financially dependent on the big three regional powers, relying on expertise and know-how from the very countries they should be seeking de facto independence from.

While Micronesian nations securing cash through direct agreements with the United States by offering the US military unlimited access to their territories, other South Pacific nations are opting for different types of dependency. Family-designated 'breadwinners' are going abroad in search of jobs to support large families back home. According to Asian Development Bank statistics, in 2002 the Kingdom of Tonga received an astonishing amount in remittances, more than $65 million, Samoa received $57.9 million and the Cook Islands $53 million. This supports a permanent brain drain. Independence is a lofty and sweet word, but little more.

Despite nationalistic rhetoric trumpeted by many governments in the region, people with skills and education are leaving, unemployment is extremely high, the standard of living, most notably in Fiji and Nauru, is declining dramatically, and due to changes in lifestyle and cheap, low-quality food imports so are peoples' health.

The creation of a New Pacific Wall has fragmented the enormous area of Oceania, once inhabited by diverse but historically intertwined cultures. There is an acute need for Pacific Island nations to construct a strong and unified bloc able to negotiate with the rest of the world as an equal partner. Only such a bloc can effectively address the political, economic, social, cultural and educational problems confronting the entire region. The people of Oceania have no choice but to look to regional solutions. The alternative can only be to continue the present dependent and humiliating order. Unfortunately, there is very little chance that such a block can be constructed in the near future.

The policies of the powers, the USA, Australia, and

New Zealand, directly thwart regional integration. *Pacnews* reported on 10 March 2009 from Brisbane:

> The former director of economic governance with the Pacific Islands Forum Secretariat has accused Australia of having a 'mean spirited' approach to trade negotiations in the region. Dr Roman Grynberg was director until last week and will now take a senior economic position with the government of Botswana in Africa. Dr Grynberg's told Radio Australia's Pacific Beat program Australia has refused to fund a position for a Chief Trade Negotiator for the Pacific Island countries leaving the region at a severe disadvantage. Dr Grynberg said "it's decisions like that which are damaging Australia's standing in the Pacific. I've always been supportive of a genuine, development agreement that provides assistance and brings all of the islands on board, not an integration with Australia and New Zealand. Pushing them into something that is going to breed bitterness in the longer term, that's not an answer and that's what they're doing now."

While Asian countries, particularly Japan, China and in some cases Taiwan and Korea, are helping to construct infrastructure, including government buildings, schools, hospitals, causeways, bridges and roads, Australia and New Zealand focus on training the army and police—the Tongan army will soon be ready to participate in 'humanitarian' missions abroad—and generally enforcing security. Japan donates ferries for short-distance travel, while Australia and New Zealand supply the region with military and police boats and patrol cars. China constructs government buildings and sports facilities, while the US, Australia and New Zealand build military compounds and police stations.

Foreign advisors from English speaking countries are now running some ministries, as well as transportation, banking and communications. The local governments are too weak to resist, often too corrupt and financially dependent on international funding, to demand more independence or a better deal for their countries.

Even with the Labor government in Canberra, the situation is definitely not improving. Policies towards Oceania of the newly elected conservative government in New Zealand have become a concern to the islanders as well as to some international organizations.

Pacnews reported on 11 March 2009:

> New Zealand foreign minister Murray McCully is spearheading a review of NZAID and has indicated his preference to change NZAID's current goal of poverty elimination to economic development...

It is time for the people of Oceania to ask whether 'aid' in its present form is seriously helping their nations, or whether it ties them down at almost no real cost to the 'donors'. In fact, they should ask whether there is any real aid at all. Those who are truly dependent on foreign 'aid' are the elites as well as the foreign contractors and advisors, but not the people who form the majority of these islands—a majority that is desperately poor in almost all countries of the region. The aid to the military and police as well as funding for 'good governance' mainly helps big players to finalize control over these fragmented islands.

As Epeli Hau'ofa pointed out, it is Oceania that is truly

aiding the rich nations including Australia, New Zealand, France and the United States. Despite their natural generosity, inhabitants of this part of the world should pause and rethink their relationships with the empire and its allies. If they still can, it would not be an easy task as they would have to attempt to change a tremendously complex and intertwined system of control. Governments and entire ruling clans benefit from preserving the status quo. But the effort is more than worthwhile—it may even be essential for the very survival of Oceania.

There will always be the sky filled with stars above the ocean full of the battered but stunningly beautiful sea creatures inhabiting it. The greed, market fundamentalism and unbridled desire to control are hopefully only passing phases in human development, while the ocean and the sky and stars are eternal. The human desire for freedom and dignity, is also eternal as is the desire for love and sharing; something that was 'normal' in the past for the sturdy and adventurous, generous and caring people of Oceania.

Some nations and cultures of Oceania may have very little time to spare. Their environment is being destroyed, resources drained, people forced to emigrate, cultures literally ravaged by neo-colonialism. The sea level is rising. Unless the people of Oceania come together as a united front to defend themselves, the world may soon lose some of its ancient, unique and diverse civilizations. Above all, the people of Oceania may lose their homes. The longer Oceania hesitates to press for unity, the higher the wall will become, and the more consolidated the system of absolute control the 'outsiders' will have over the region and its people.

The Cultures of Oceania—
PAST, PRESENT AND FUTURE

I am tired
Of being naive
Talking to myself
Winding handless clocks
And bailing the ocean
Tomorrow
I shall go
To church, the police station
Parliament house, the courts
Other corridors and the market
Places
They say
Where you can buy truth easily.

['Home at Last', Epeli Hau'ofa]

I T IS OFTEN PERCEIVED THAT STORY TELLING IN OCEANIA is based on oral tradition and that the written word is alien to many cultures in this vast region of seemingly endless ocean, dotted by thousands of islands.

But there is a striking paradox: while most of the countries of Oceania do not have a single bookstore worthy of the name—even Samoa with over 180,000 inhabitants has only Christian book stores it passes as 'bookshops', Oceania has given birth to several brave, innovative, even brilliant novelists, poets and non-fiction writers. Almost all of them write in English as local languages, it is said, are not always fitting for novels or poetry forms.

Native writers have not always been admired or acclaimed at home; Samoan novelist Albert Wendt for example, has faced difficulties in publishing and distributing his work in his native country. But it is a fact that men and women of letters from all over Oceania are greatly enriching contemporary world literature and most of those who do are, above all, great storytellers, bringing together imported form and local substance. Moreover, the literature of Oceania pulls no punches, and in this respect, no other art form in the Pacific rivals it in addressing social problems.

Albert Wendt has offered a mirror to the often frightening face of Samoan culture in one of his best known works, the beautifully crafted novella and book of short stories *Flying Fox in a Freedom Tree*. His compatriot, Sia Figiel, in her powerful novel, *Where We Once Belonged*, described the brutality of growing up in an oppressive Samoan family. Her book was recently put on stage and described by Auckland Theatre Company artistic director, Colin McColl as:

...a coming of age story in Samoa that Margaret

Mead could never have imagined. Brave, brutal, unflinchingly honest and very, very funny, it has the same innocent perspective on a chaotic rite of passage as *Mister Pip* or *The Kite Runner.*

In his fiction, Joseph Veramu, the leading Fijian educator, describes marginal youths growing up in misery and confusion, in the slums far from the flashy international hotels and resorts his country is renowned for. His story 'The Toothache', for instance, depicted several disasters Fiji is presently facing, from racial intolerance and military coups to the collapsing social system and poverty.

In his brilliant, outrageous and hilarious novel *Kisses in the Nederends*, Papuan born Tongan/Fijian writer and anthropologist Epeli Hau'ofa draws parallels between the pain in his rectum and the complexities of living in Polynesian society. His 'Tales of the Tikongs' depicts, in a series of anecdotes and stories, the uneasy cohabitation between traditional cultures of Oceania and implanted neocolonial structures. In a powerful and poetic non-fiction book, *We Are The Ocean*, Epeli Hau'ofa attempted to redefine Pacific (Oceania) along its historic and cultural lines.

Oceania has talented poets and one of the best of them is the Tongan Konai Helu Thaman. Her poems are not only elegantly crafted; they describe dilemmas faced by Oceania, its struggles and insecurities, as well as its history and traditional knowledge.

thinking is tiring
like paddling against the waves
until feeling comes lightly
late into the pacific night

when the islands calm me
stroking my sorrows
i ask for silence
and they give it
i ask for forgiveness
and they raise my face

France Mugler and John Lynch of the University of the South Pacific compare indigenous oral traditions:

> The South Pacific has a rich oral tradition in its many indigenous languages, a multifarious tradition where performance is central and which ranges from story telling to epic poetry and genealogies, oratory, songs, and drama. Literacy, introduced by missionaries in the Nineteenth Century, spread fairly quickly and many South Pacific languages—though far from all, given their very large number—were soon written. But most literature in English about the South Pacific was for a long time written by outsiders (among them Herman Melville, Robert Louis Stevenson, Pierre Loti, Jack London, Somerset Maugham and James Michener), with 'outsiders' points of view, so that places and people were by turns romanticised, demonised, or simply marginalised.

In their view, indigenous written literature began to emerge in the postwar era, and especially from the 1960s:

> Except for a few early works, such as *Miss Ulysses of Puka Puka*, an autobiographical story by the Cook Islander Florence ('Johnny') Frisbie in 1948, literature

in English by South Pacific Islanders did not emerge until the 1960s.

In 1960, perhaps the first novel by South Pacific Island writers was published, *Makutu*, by the Cook Islanders Tom and Lydia Davis. The late 1960s and early 1970s saw the first works of a number of writers: short stories by Fiji's Raymond Pillai and Subramani and Tonga's 'Epeli Hau'ofa; poems by Konai Helu Thaman of Tonga, and Fiji's Pio Manoa (who also often writes in Fijian); and short stories, poems and, in 1973, the novel *Sons for the Return Home*, by the Samoan Albert Wendt, of all South Pacific writers perhaps the best known outside the region.

But every year, new works of fiction emerge. Just to mention a few of the most important writers: Kauraka Kauraka, a poet from the Cook Islands, Vilsoni Hereniko, a Rotuman/Fijian playwright, John Pule, Niuenan artist, novelist and poet, and Vincent Eri, author of the first Papua New Guinean novel *The Crocodile*.

And on the naughtier side, no list would be complete without Bob Browne and his *Grassroots*—a manga series, depicting, ridiculing and trashing almost all the major problems Papua New Guinea is presently facing. Its hilarious dialogue is not written in the Queens English:

> Eh, mai fren... you's a veri fortunit person hindeed! Holding in your han is wan veri spesel buk.. Dis buk it's not like ol the other wans they bin raiting on the Papua New Guinea Pidgin.. Oh no.. This wan it's not 4 the hakademikals studying the lenguage 4 hakwiring the pepa kwalifickesens like the Ph.D. or gred 10 setifiket...

Nogat tru!! Dis buk it's 4 the veri prektials.. pipols like you an' mi.. The real grass roots.. Em nau!! So when yous opening it be redi 4 gut taim of your laif dying of the lafters.. mai fren, you gotta laf... speselly if yous living in Papua New Guinea!!! An' if yous not hekspiriens the laif in P.N.G. yet, you mas kam -- speselly if yous rich forin bisnisman... kam an' visit mi, an' bring your big sekbuk an' i'll be giving you the veri spesel pesonel lessons in talkign the pidgin!!! Sapos you no inap kam, sori.. Send the moni eniway!!

But it certainly captures vibrant PNG!

In Oceania, there are several different ways to tell a story and none of them seem to be 'above' the others in terms of hierarchy: traditional story telling in Oceania was done verbally or through elaborate storyboards, some of the most impressive and complete coming from the Micronesian nation of Palau.

The reason for so few bookstores? One of them is that knowledge and public property somehow don't go together in the mind of the people in this part of the world. Ms. Konai Helu Thaman explains that there is no culture of buying books:

"People bring the book from somewhere and then they borrow it from each other so dozens read the same book."

WHAT CONSTITUTES OCEANIA'S CULTURES?

The perception of culture in Oceania is often different from that in the Western world or even East Asia where most of the Oceanic civilizations come from originally. Here, you will search in vain for monumental opera houses and concert halls, for Presidential libraries and film festivals. Culture in Oceania is what you see: the lifestyle that local people live.

Culture can be reflected in an outrigger canoe with its crew smoothly paddling through the harbors and bays of the Cook Islands and Samoa; it can be a long tale about some wise fish or horror stories of cannibalism that occurred generations ago in the Solomon Islands, Fiji or Papua New Guinea. Culture can be expressed by traditional protocol and ceremonies of welcome, as well as in the tattoos on the bodies of Samoan or French Polynesian men and women. The entire kava (the local mildly intoxicating drink) ceremony in Tonga and elsewhere is considered part of the culture; as is betel nut chewing all over Micronesia and Papua New Guinea. Culture is Sunday's combination of traditional lava-lava (skirt), bleached shirt and tie worn by Samoan men on the way to church, and it can be the way children of Oceania are treated by their parents (not always a pretty sight) or the great respect that is shown to elders. Culture is what is behind the still continuing epic drama of eerie fallen idols—Moais— dotting the coast of Isla de Pascua (Easter Island). Culture is also the cult of Fafafine—men, particularly in Samoa, who are from childhood dressed like women and behave like women, but who are not necessarily gay.

There are certainly many elements of modernity in the culture of almost all countries of Oceania, including an increased accent on tangibility. Papua New Guinea and Vanuatu, artistically one of the most creative nations in the Pacific, which with significant foreign influence, built impressive National Museums. Port Vila in Vanuatu reserved an entire huge field, more suitable than an enclosed theatre, argued local artists, for its elaborate dances and other cultural performances. Almost every country in the region records compact discs with its classical and contemporary music. However, the culture almost everywhere in Oceania is still deeply rooted in traditional perceptions and forms.

"We don't have culture necessarily linked to the arts, as in the West," explains Ms. Konai Helu Thaman. "But what exactly is our culture in Oceania? First of all, I don't think there is only one culture. My definition of culture follows very much that of UNESCO which looks at a way of life of the people, what they are doing and how they are thinking. Oceania, in my interpretation, is embracing culture, but it is very difficult to pinpoint, because within that there are many different cultural groups and their thinking and acting is closely linked to their languages. And we have hundreds of languages here."

"Epeli's vision of Oceania is very philosophical," Ms. Konai Helu Thaman refers to the recently deceased Tongan thinker and writer Epeli Hau'ofa. "It has to do with identity and belonging to Oceania, which isn't necessarily a geographic place—I think he is talking about a state of mind. And I agree—it is a state of mind, although I am still struggling to define it. According to UNESCO, Oceania consists of Pacific islands plus Australia and New Zealand. The state of mind Epeli is talking about is different for each individual. You have your own notion of what that is; I have my own ... But I suspect that there are many people in Australia and New Zealand who don't have any notion at all. Then, what do I share with someone from Perth or Tasmania? I lived in New Zealand for years and I worked with many Australians. I understand New Zealand but most of them don't understand Tonga. The inclusiveness of Epeli's theory is good, but I think that unless you lived in Tonga or Samoa or the Solomon Islands or elsewhere on the Pacific islands, irrespective of where you are from, you can't understand us. And there are people like yourself or my husband who are from Europe or America. They live here and share our culture and are part of us; they understand and appreciate things here while people from neighboring countries have no clue about what we are all about."

Of course the 'neighboring countries' are having a great influence on Oceania. Aid money comes with strings attached. Children of Oceania educated in the US, Australia and New Zealand often come back with values diametrically opposed to those traditionally respected in this part of the world. The erosion of local culture, at least to some degree, is inevitable.

"There is no doubt that Pacific cultures are being eroded by outside forces, like globalization and integration," explains Visesio Pongi, UNESCO head for Oceania. "That is why the Pacific islands must be strategic about how they approach their own culture. It is not good enough to preserve or safeguard them as if cultures were only confined to museums or cultural centers. In the case of the Pacific, cultures are manifest more in the form of the 'intangible' rather than the 'tangible.' Pacific islands must find a way to use their traditions, customs and practices as a means to move forward, for their own sustainable development. Only then can they survive and thrive, and give meaning to the Pacific cultures as such."

There are hundreds of examples of the determined struggle of local cultures to survive, but there are also hundreds of tragic cases of culture disappearing.

"Look at some small islands", exclaims Emily Waterman,

Australian cultural consultant in the Pacific. "I recently spent time on a small island in a Pacific country." Emily went on to speak about a unique local dance that was performed by the men of this community. However, it had not been performed for around 15 years, and is close to being lost from this community as only the elders remember the dance; the younger generations have never seen it performed.

"There are also cases where some of the traditional games children grew up playing have now disappeared from memory and practice. While some ceremonies and cultural elements are still practiced by families and these communities, she fears that influences from outside—DVDs and migration to the capital cities of overseas countries are so great that unique cultures in small island communities may only survive for a few more generations."

Oceania has some of the greatest cultural diversity in the world. Papua New Guinea alone has over 850 known local languages, which is over one tenth of the world's total. There are 74 languages in the Solomon Islands, 70 of which are still living. Even the tiniest countries like Tuvalu have their own mother tongue. Niue, the country with the smallest population in the world—1,444 according to the last count—speaks its own language, Niuean, and it recently published the first-ever monolingual dictionary of its tongue: truly a remarkable achievement!

Even in the Western sense of culture (as almost synonymous to art) Oceania, given its small population of less than 10 million people, excels.

Some of the world's greatest art museums and galleries—from the Metropolitan Museum of Art in New York City to the Musee du Quai Branly in Paris—now permanently exhibit outriggers, roof carvings, masks and totems from Oceania.

And in late 2008 and early 2009 some of Switzerland's most prestigious museums are offering a profusion of traditional masks and other artwork from Oceania along with well-known European classical paintings.

In some parts of Oceania, culture and art are still an inseparable part of life.

While the government of Tuvalu is busy evacuating people from the outer islands due to rising seas, local people have their own way to resist, to boost their morale and defy the polluters and politicians responsible for the destruction of nature: they perform powerful and spectacular traditional dances. Each atoll has different dances. Arguably one of the most stunning is from the Funafuti Atoll and is called Fatele. It is an event performed only on special occasions. The performers are divided into two competing groups showing their art consecutively in a large assembly hall. Each group is comprised of dozens of dancers dressed in banana leaves and straw skirts with women dancing and men drumming by smashing their fists against short legged wooden tables.

There are spectacular dances devoted to all occasions—from wars to weddings to wakes—in Vanuatu, the Solomon Islands, Fiji, Tonga, Samoa, Papua New Guinea, Kiribati, the Cook Islands and elsewhere. Kiribati offers a rainbow of brilliant dances, chants and original rhythms, some performed and sung in traditional dwellings—maneabas—just for the joy of the local people themselves. Another impressive dance form is the Lakalaka from Tonga. This was proclaimed a masterpiece of intangible cultural heritage, by UNESCO in 2005.

To the great regret of the purists, several countries are now trying to convert these great traditional cultural events into tourist attractions. All five-star resorts in Fiji offer dance performances, some on a nightly basis. So do several up-market establishments in Tahiti, French Polynesia, Samoa and the Cook Islands. The Samoan fire dance is legendary, as are the war dances of Vanuatu. While many of these performances are absolutely legitimate, the ambience and choreography of others don't necessarily dwell on pure local culture.

The finest musical and dance expressions in Oceania are still taking place on the remote atolls and islands, far away from tourist centers and resorts where fusion has replaced the original spiritual-art form.

Ron Crocombe in his *The South Pacific* explains:

> Early forms of music, dance, drama and decorative arts have not been well preserved, and knowledge of these arts before contact with industrial technology is patchy. Song and dance were universal, but much of it was suppressed by early missionaries because it was sexually explicit or aggressive. Some such dances disappeared, others continued in clandestine parties that spread after sailors in the 1800s introduced alcohol and techniques to make it. European traditions influenced music more than dance.

New Cultures of Oceania

The Church, a colonial implant, tried to monopolize cultural and artistic expressions for some time, but eventually, mainly after several countries of Oceania gained independence, traditional art forms regained prominence, although often in modified form.

Art rarely, if ever, survives in its traditional form. Oceania is no exception. Modern art is always evolving, seeking fusion and trying to incorporate itself into the wider world without losing its essence and identity. There are great examples of creative musical production in Papua New Guinea (PNG), strongly influenced by Caribbean reggae and even rap, but also by tribal musical forms from all corners of that extremely diverse country. Countless clubs in Port Moresby offer the stage to local bands, and radio stations blast original fusion genres over the airways. PNG has produced world-famous artists, including Sanguma and George Telek who have been touring and working in Europe and Australia. Ben Hakalitz and Baruka Tau performed with Yothu Yindi in stadiums in Brazil and closed the 2000 Sydney Olympics.

Vanuatu, Samoa, Tonga, Cook Islands, Solomon Islands and other countries of Oceania have their own music groups and often original music style, mostly fusion, although less avant-garde than that of PNG.

Oceania has centuries of experience with the visual arts, although before the contact with the outside world local visual artists mainly concentrated on wood carving elaborate canoes, the roofs and ceilings of houses and bais, totems, masks, as well as textiles.

Gauguin began the trend of foreign, mostly European, painters traveling to Oceania and settling, a trend that continues today with such artists as Russian painter Nicolai Michoutouchkine and his partner Aloi Pilioko, two of Oceania's best known practicing artists living in Port Vila, the capital of Vanuatu, who set up a foundation for the preservation of artistic values in the Pacific region, and French painter and sculptor Garrick Yrondi who settled in Bora Bora, French Polynesia.

Although Hawaii and New Zealand are still the two main hubs for artists from Oceania in terms of publishing and the frequency of exhibitions, there are now some major cultural institutions on the islands themselves. One of the most impressive is the Jean-Marie Tjibaou Cultural Centre in New Caledonia designed by renowned Italian architect Renzo Piano, which offers art workshops, exhibits traditional art from all over Oceania, as well as contemporary works like those of John Pule. Another two, more modestly funded, but vibrant and creative institutions, are the Oceania Centre for Arts and Culture at the University of the South Pacific (U.S.P.) in Suva, Fiji, and previously run by Epeli Hau'ofa, and the Vanuatu Cultural Center in Port Vila, Vanuatu, renowned for its live performance of 'sand drawing' which UNESCO proclaimed a masterpiece of intangible cultural heritage in 2005.

Museums are not up to world standards and are grossly under funded, but there is at least one in each independent country, the most significant ones being in Port Moresby (PNG), Suva (Fiji), Vila (Vanuatu).

There are also many talented visual artists with no institutional base, who draw on materials available from their native lands. PNG poet and painter Purago Marabe is one of them. Probably the most famous PNG artist is Mathias Kauage, a man from a humble Miugu Village in the highlands of Simbu Province, who conquered the world with his disarming, simple style of magical figures and creatures, some of them drawn from PNG legends and tales. His work can be found in Africa as well as in Europe— one of his paintings decorated Buckingham Palace where he was honored with an O.B.E. by Queen Elizabeth in 1998. There is also the eccentric Samoan sculptor Penehuro Papalii with his enormous studio and workshop full of rusting car carcasses, wooden statues of talking chiefs, and metal bars, whose work was commissioned by China just before the Beijing Olympics.

Intangible heritage may be the backbone of Oceania, but some important tangible heritage can also be found all over the region. Rapa Nui (Isla de Pascua or Easter Island) with its cities built on the rim of a crater, caverns with drawings and enormous sculptures called moai, is one of the most impressive historical sites of ancient Oceania. At the time of writing, it is still the only UNESCO cultural world Heritage Site in Oceania, although there are several candidates nearly ready to be approved. It is followed by the mysterious historical empire/cities in the Federated States of Micronesia (FSM); Nan Madol on the island of Pohnpei and Lelu the walled city on the island of Kosrae. Both would long ago have been declared world heritage sites if they were not located on private property and therefore in disputed land areas.

There is impressive local architecture in Palau, from traditional wooden houses, 'bais', to entire hills shaped like Borobudur temples in Java, as well as bizarre archeological areas covered by erected stones and sculptures (not unlike Rapa Nui). And with more than 800 hundred cultures, Papua New Guinea is home to abundant distinct rural architectural styles.

There are a number of recent architectural structures of note built in the last two centuries, ranging from the first Fijian capital city of Levuka on the small island of Ovalau, to historic parts of Vila (Vanuatu), Apia (Samoa), Nuka'Alofa in Tonga, and Hindu and Muslim temples built by Indo-Fijians all over the Fijian Islands. Probably the iconic building of Oceania is the National Parliament

House in Port Moresby, PNG, opened in 1984.

The diversity of the tangible heritage of Oceania is tremendous—but perhaps the true richness of the cultures of the region lie in its intangible forms. One of the most powerful symbols of this is the sand drawing of Vanuatu: an artist creates one masterpiece at a time—in one continuous movement they engrave precise and elegant lines into sand placed on a framed board. It contains secret codes and messages. People watch as the artist works. They watch while the work is completed. Then with one sharp movement of the artist's hands, the board is shaken and the entire artwork disappears. What is left is once again an even surface of white sand enclosed by the wooden frame. Each artwork lives for only few seconds. What matters is the process, not the result. And its perfection is to remain engraved in peoples' memories, not in a material world of impermanence.

EDUCATION, CULTURE AND SURVIVAL

Languages, traditions, and arts: all of them essential for Oceania, all are part of the culture. But none could survive on its own, without what is now shaping so positively and negatively this entire part of the world: education.

Education is essential for Oceania to survive and gain true independence. Education is bringing to Oceania new concepts and perceptions, new knowledge. It is both a bridge and a battleground: certainly it is among the most sensitive and contested issues in the Pacific. What kinds of education would be most appropriate? What mix of formal and informal? Should curricula be based on those of former colonial powers, or should Oceania build on its own traditional knowledge? Is it capable of choosing its own curricula? Would it be allowed to do so?

"Traditionally, people in Pacific Islands consider education and learning as the most important key for a better livelihood and future," explains Yayoi Segi who worked in Oceania for UNESCO as an education adviser. "Learning has always taken place at home and in the village. Passing down of knowledge and life skills from generation to generation as relevant to the way of living in a particular household and village has been widely practiced and is the responsibility of village chiefs and the elderly. This way of informal education and learning has played a significant role in the safeguarding of family, village, and ultimately national heritage in countries where intangible forms of culture are rich yet are being eroded due to the rapidly encroaching forces of globalization and regional integration across the Pacific."

"Nowadays, when it comes to education and learning, most talk of schooling, and investment is concentrated on basic education covering the first 6 to 8 years of schooling. In their respective National Constitutions, the governments attach paramount importance to education and learning as a critical means to nation building and sustainable development. Governments regularly allocate 18 to 25 percent of the state budget to education, most of which goes to basic education covering primary and part of secondary schooling. Most Pacific Island countries have achieved impressive levels of access to basic education with more than 90 percent for both boys and girls in primary education in urban, rural and outer island settings."

Not all, of course, as there is, for instance, Papua New Guinea that is fairing much worse. As Ms. Segi correctly points out: "Comparatively speaking, most Pacific Island countries are among the better performing countries because of their success in nearly universalizing primary education. However, there is acute lack of data or statistics that enable them to analyse how to improve their education systems, such as evidence-based policy, planning, implementation and monitoring and evaluation. With limited availability of data, one can consider those the three principal challenges facing the countries right now."

Most countries now use two languages for instruction— the local tongue and the language of the former or present colonial power: basically English or French, and Spanish on Rapa Nui, (which is a Chilean territory).

Most information about the outside world comes from local newspapers, radio stations and meager TV offerings. Some satellite providers carry only one New Zealand or Australian channel, BBC World, FOX and or CNN as well as one local channel. Foreign interests, mainly those from Australia, control most of the media but there is even one newspaper in PNG—*The National*—that is owned by a Malaysian logging conglomerate. For a long time, Pacific academics and intellectuals have warned of ideological indoctrination by the regional powers.

Pacific Way—a pan-Oceania regionalist intellectual movement (which in part wanted to revitalize common aspects of Pacific culture, including decision making through consensus and dialogue, rather than confrontation)—as well as Marxism (both popular at U.S.P. and elsewhere among educated youth in the late 70s) were destroyed or manipulated to extinction, by internal and external forces.

In his book *We are the Ocean* Epeli Hau'ofa wrote:

> The development of a clear regional identity within this university [U.S.P.] was also hampered by the introduction in the early 1980s of neo-Marxism, which, as a global movement, was quite hostile to any expression of localism and regionalism. According to this ideology, Pacific people were part of a worldwide class structure based on an international division of labour. Nationalism and regionalism were bourgeois attempts to prevent the international unity of the working classes. The demise of the Pacific Way through natural causes—and the disappearance of neo-Marxism as a direct result of the 1987 right-wing military coup in Fiji—removed from our campus discourses on ideologies that transcended cultural diversity.

Konai Helu Thaman confirms this: "Of course, the 70s and 80s were when students at U.S.P. were so active ... There were marches, meetings, and discussions ... We were called a hotbed of Marxism ... It has all stopped now ..."

Western political 'teaching', often simply promoting dominant neo-liberal ideologies through the funding of educational programs, certain types of scholarships, control of mass media and direct propaganda gigs, was extremely 'successful.' Today, there is almost no political diversity in Oceania, except in the Chilean territory of Rapa Nui and, paradoxically, in the French colonies. There is enforced consensus on the supremacy of market economics for Oceania despite the fact that it is in direct contradiction with collective and social cultural traditions of Oceania, generally hostile feelings towards China, which is another paradox, as China provides a number of nations of Oceania with sound aid programs, and admiration for the United States and its international military adventures. Thus politicians from Oceania consistently support almost all US foreign policy decisions and this never evokes serious outcry at home.

"A big problem is heavy reliance on external assistance as linked to capacity and governance," explained Yayoi Segi. "Traditionally, Australia, New Zealand and the US have provided significant financial resources. This is often tied to the use of materials and the hiring of advisors and consultants who may not be aware of local context and end up providing support of little relevance or value. This aspect is inevitably linked to capacity and governance. A paper written by Hilda Heine and Emi Chutaro of RMI revealed a strong correlation between increasing US financial aid and decreasing control of the education system on the part of Marshallese."

"In my opinion, countries are chronically dependent on external sources partially because they are running a system that is modeled after, or is identical to, the Western form of schooling. First, they need to build schools that are child friendly with all sorts of facilities. Why not use existing infrastructure instead? Secondly, teacher and principal training and development is a continuous process and costly. Thirdly, the procurement and distribution of materials such as textbooks and resource books is expensive, too, let alone training teachers on how to use them. Why use textbooks? The former Minister of Education in Palau, Mario Katosang, once passionately told me that learning should take place outside the classroom and school setting. Teachers can take their students to the beach to study the composition and erosion of sand, as well as the physical environment surrounding the beach. Maths and language arts can be incorporated into that, too. Why are textbooks needed? Living resources that bear testimony to what life is all about surround children."

Among educators there seems to be a consensus that Oceania needs its own curricula and that local knowledge should be an inseparable part of the learning process. Former Minister of Education of Palau, Mario Katosang, is one of the main promoters of such an approach: "Several years ago I visited an experimental school that was teaching children from Palau, as well as several foreign students, mainly from Asia, right on the shore of the ocean, using surrounding trees, coral, creatures and plants, tools and objects of interest. On the southern island of Peleliu, the location of one of the bloodiest battles between the US and Japanese forces during WWII, an entire school, the largest building on the island, has been converted to a community center, a communication hub with free computers and internet for all villagers after school hours, a library, as well as a music and cultural center, dramatically improving standards of living on the island."

Many see Palau's approach as 'experimental', but in reality

it is just a return to its own cultural roots; a return that is not encouraged in most of the other countries of Oceania.

"The curriculum that we are using is a legacy of British colonial days," explains Teekoa Ietaake, the outspoken Permanent Secretary of Education of Kiribati. "Almost nothing has changed since then. We try to implement some elements of traditional values. We are making attempts to promote local culture. But we can't isolate ourselves from the larger world and therefore can't avoid influences from Australia and New Zealand. Why the West? Formal education was not part of our culture and colonial masters introduced it to us. And our oldest educators were students of the colonial masters, that's why …"

Three hours away by plane, in Suva, Fiji, Konaii Helu Thaman agrees: "The curriculum in our schools is just lifted from the curriculums of schools in the UK, Australia and New Zealand, or from the United States, and reforms that would put an accent on our culture and traditions are not encouraged from abroad. You see, no educational reform in the Pacific can be done without donors. And with donors come foreign consultants. We have of course, people on different islands who try to bring these points out. But mostly they are silenced. It is our culture, anyway, that if someone comes and gives you money, you don't question what they tell you. You have to be polite."

The result is that many educators in Oceania remain frustrated by the influence from abroad, the brain drain, and a culture that is no longer passed from generation to generation. However, there seems to be a resistance and a growing consensus that Oceania has to fight back—it has to regain its voice and its way of life, its culture. There may be no political unity but many are preparing, at least individually and in the context of their own countries, to fight back for the survival of their culture. As a counterbalance, Konaii Helu Thaman developed an indigenous research methodology called Kakala. Joseph Veramu explains: "Kakala is a traditional Tongan fragrant flower. The model synthesizes the best of Pacific and Western heritage and learning and it helps to move us forward."

Not everything is rosy on the islands surrounded by white beaches, coral reefs and turquoise waters. Culture may be old and deep, but it can also be oppressive. Real crimes, real abuse, real oppression is often hiding behind that simple and noble word 'culture'. Much is, as in any old culture, simply deplorable.

But Oceania and its culture (or more precisely, its cultures) can still offer much to the world and to its own people, even if the offering should come in moderated and in more progressive form. The enormous space inhabited by Oceania people gives them a certain kind of generosity rarely seen elsewhere. It gives them the ability to dream and to see far—almost beyond the horizon; it gives them tranquility and security and often a lack of fear. The beauty they grew up with can hardly be matched by that in any other part of the world. For others, *por mares nunca dantes navegados*, for men and women of Oceania—home.

In the 21st Century, storytelling, as beautiful as it is, will not suffice to protect endangered culture. Epeli Hau'ofa knew it. In 2009 he died fighting till the end for the conversations concerning the intangible and the tangible, the perishable and the permanent. He believed in Oceania and he believed in the creative forces of this part of the world. It is therefore with his firm voice that I conclude this chapter:

It is essential for us in Oceania that the creative arts and other forms of cultural production take up what our formal educational institutions have marginalized as nonessential in the world of the twenty-first century. For us they are necessary tools for the attainment and maintenance of autonomy within a homogenizing global system. Our social, economic, and political institutions are woven into the larger world system; any free space within will have to be established though creative cultural production. And this is what the present and rising generations of Oceania's growing and widely dispersed intelligentsia are furiously involved in today. From their far-flung bases in Guam, California, Hawai'i, Cook Islands, New Zealand, Fiji, Samoa, Tonga, Solomon Islands, Papua New Guinea, Australia, and increasingly elsewhere within and beyond the Pacific Basin, they are connecting through the Internet and face-to-face encounters to discuss and work towards a culturally creative and free Oceania.

The Tragedy of the Marshall Islands:
NUCLEAR EXPERIMENTS AND THE KWAJALEIN MISSILE RANGE

E JIT ISLAND MAY BE JUST A STONE'S THROW FROM Majuro, the main island of the Republic of the Marshall Islands (RMI), but it feels isolated and abandoned. Many inhabitants live in the past, survivors of US nuclear experiments remembering their real home abandoned decades ago. Ejit was supposed to be just a short stop, a transit point, not a permanent destination.

"There are documents which indicate that our people had to survive nuclear experiments, particularly on Rongelap Atoll," explains Alson J. Kelen from the Marshall Island's Council of NGOs. "To me, these were long term experiments on humans. The United States also performed psychological tests on us, moving our people from one atoll to another."

We sit in Mr. Kelen's simple but cozy home on Ejit Island, surrounded by his wife and children. To get to Ejit I had to drive to the tip of Majuro, park my car, and then walk across the coral reef with the water up to my knees. My feet and calves are bruised, despite wearing and ruining a pair of leather shoes.

"The compensation we get from the United States is not enough," continues Mr. Kelen. "Right now, the situation is quite confusing. Bikini is not yet ready for us, for returnees, but the US wants to pull the plug—stop helping displaced Bikini citizens. Bikini is not yet clean; it is still radioactive. While it is safe to make a short visit, it would be deadly to live there. Divers go, but they don't eat the fish from around the island. Eventually, most of us would love to go back."

Numerous nuclear weapons tests were conducted by the USA in Micronesia, primarily on the Bikini Atoll where 23 nuclear devices were exploded, from 1946 through 1958. On March 1, 1954, the Castle Bravo hydrogen bomb test generated radioactive fallout and contaminated Rongelap Atoll, located 150 miles from Bikini. Rongelap Atoll consisted of 61 islets with a combined land area of 8 sq km. Three days after the test, the inhabitants, with their distinctive and ancient culture, were forced to abandon their homes, leaving all their belongings. They were subsequently sent to Kwajalein for medical treatment and 'observation'.

Based on its official communiques, internet site and face-to-face conversations, this is how Greenpeace describes the events:

Since 1945 most of the world has lived in fear of nuclear war, but for many Pacific Islanders from 1948 to 1956, nuclear war was a reality. In the 8 years of atmospheric nuclear testing at Bikini Atoll, fallout from 66 fission and hydrogen bombs rained down on their region.

On March 1, 1954, the United States exploded a hydrogen bomb, code named 'Bravo'. At 15 megatons 'Bravo' was a thousand times more powerful than 'Little Boy' the bomb dropped on Hiroshima, and after the explosion there was a marked increase in the level of background radiation measured around the globe.

The inhabitants of Bikini and Enewetak were evacuated from their island homes prior to the nuclear tests to avoid exposure to radioactive fallout. But the inhabitants of Rongelap 150 kilometres away, were not so fortunate.

Within four hours of the explosion, fallout from Bravo was settling on the island. A fine white ash landed on the heads and bare arms of people standing in the open. It dissolved into water supplies and drifted into houses.

The snow-like debris fell all day and into the evening, covering the ground up to 2 centimetres thick. On the day after the blast, Americans wearing protective suits came to the island. They took readings with a Geiger counter from two wells and left after 20 minutes, without saying a word, according to the islanders.

Although American authorities knew of the fallout pattern and the strong winds that had been blowing towards Rongelap on the day of the test, they made no attempt to evacuate the Islanders for more than 48 hours. Many Marshallese believe the Rongelap Islanders were used by the US as 'guinea pigs' to study the effects of radioactive fallout on humans. Scientists at the Brookhaven National Laboratory in New York State stated that "The habitation of these people on the island will afford most valuable ecological radiation data on human beings."

The USA declared Rongelap 'clean and safe' in 1957, encouraging the islanders to return. As many residents developed thyroid-tumors and many children died of leukemia evidence of continued contamination mounted, this caused a certain embarrassment to the US government. The magistrate of Rongelap, John Anjain, whose son died of leukemia, made international appeals for help, but the plight of the islanders has been generally ignored.

Greenpeace helped to evacuate the people from Rongelap in 1985 and assisted their resettlement on the islets of Mejatto and Ebeye on Kwajalein Atoll, ironically a stone's throw from the US-leased Kwajalein Missile Range. Ebeye is one of the most overcrowded islands in Oceania and it is significantly smaller than the islands of Rongelap. After resettlement, it began suffering from pollution as it is a dumping ground for the US military base at Kwajalein. It also suffered un-employment, an extremely high suicide rate, and inad-equate medical care, clean water and electricity supply.

Back in Ejit, Mr. Kelen suggested several solutions: "Elderly people want to go back—they want to die where they came from. Some younger people don't want to return. Until Bikini is ready for us again, they want to move from the small land they were given to the bigger land in the US It would also be helpful if the US didn't just give us frozen and canned food. And if they gave us good teachers, we the Bikinians would be able to become good doctors, lawyers, and chefs. What is done is done. Now, either clean up the place or give us some other land where we can go and live permanently."

The resettlement project of Ejit Atoll dates back to the 1970s. Most of the homes were built here with US aid. There are hardly any job opportunities—inhabitants of the atoll have to commute daily to Majuro by boat when the tide is high or on foot when it is low, negotiating the sharp surfaces of the coral. Despite the passage of time, the settlement still feels like a temporary solution. Many inhabitants are waiting for the opportunity to go home or to move to some more attractive part of the world. As the quarrelsome negotiations between the US government and the displaced people and their children continue, elderly refugees are dying, while others still in the prime of life are falling ill as a consequence of the nuclear experiments that occurred many decades ago.

The official site of the Bikini Atoll declares:

> While most people tend to mark time with clocks and calendars, we, the people of Bikini, tend to take measure of our own lives each time one of our elders dies.

With the elders dying in exile, the unique culture of Bikini is gradually disappearing. That is something that will not be possible to correct with any amount of compensation. So far the United States has paid the lump sum of $150 million as settlement for damages caused by the nuclear testing program, a pittance compared to the several billions needed for compensation and cleanup, according to experts.

This is a part of a damning *j'accuse* from 'A pronouncement on a United Church of Christ ministry and witness with Micronesians':

> The US government has not played fair in the com-

pensation paid to the Marshallese peoples, nor in the information given to the affected communities.

This came to light when people of Bikini were told that it was safe to return to Bikini. Experts demonstrated how radiation levels could be lowered to 'scientifically-acceptable levels'—an annual exposure of 100 millirems per person—as long as people avoided eating large amounts of local food.

While Bikinians were told that 100 millirems per person was safe, the US Environmental Protection Agency (EPA) had quietly adopted a 15-millirem standard for the resettlement of radiologically contaminated sites in the United States. This 15 millirem standard has recently been adopted for the Marshall Islands, but only after the attorney for Enewetak Atoll, Davor Pevec, found out about the EPA standard for US residents.

This double standard—subjecting the Bikinians to six times the safe level as determined by the EPA—is also seen in the compensation levels. While Congress has spent $12 billion in Hanford, California, without even putting a shovel in the ground for environmental cleanup there, Bikini has only received $90 million thus far from the United States for cleanup.

Recently declassified US nuclear test studies show that 22 atolls—not just the four atolls mentioned for compensation in the Compact: Rongelap, Enewetak, Utrik, and Bikini—received nuclear test fallout above maximum permissible safety levels. This information was not provided to Marshall Islands negotiators when the Compact of Free Association, with its $150 million nuclear compensation to survivors, was agreed upon in 1983.

While greater compensation was given to American citizens living downwind of the Nevada Test Site as a one-time lump sum, amounting to a billion dollars, the $150 million was not adequate to cover the claims filed by the victims of radiation poisoning in the RMI. Approximately $7 billion of compensation claims are still languishing in the US courts today and most victims who have been compensated have been compensated only partially and in small monthly payments.

It seems to be fair to state that the compensation scheme was not only inadequate, but it also failed to attempt to find any integrated solution to the plight of the affected people. Delaying further compensation payments meant large savings for the US government, as addressed in the following part of this chilling announcement:

Fully one third of the 1,574 Marshall Islands recipients of nuclear test awards have died without receiving full compensation. The Marshall Island government is asking, in the renegotiation of the Compact of Free Association, for an additional $2.7 billion for damage caused by American nuclear testing. When seen in the light of $12 billion for Hanford (just for environmental cleanup), the amount being requested by RMI is very modest. No amount of money will ever compensate for the suffering of the Marshallese people; however, an amount equivalent to or more than the $12 billion spent on cleanup at Hanford would be more just.

The US is now trying to stop lawsuits arising out of

the irradiation of the Marshallese from being heard in court. The Compact of Free Association contains an espousal clause, stipulating that the US has paid a lump sum of $150 million for damages and from now on all responsibility falls on the shoulders of RMI. This unjust clause in the Compact must be overturned in the light of classified information that was not made available to RMI negotiators at the time the Compact was being negotiated and which now reveals the real extent of the testing and the fact that Marshall Islanders were knowingly put at risk during the Bravo test.

More than $2 billion in awards to Marshall Islanders for personal injuries and land damage and nuclear clean ups has already been approved, but the Majuro-based Nuclear Claims Tribunal announced in December 2008 that it would not provide any compensation payments in 2008, as it had no funds to disperse.

Giff Johnson reported in his article No Compensation for N-Test Victims in 2008 (*Pacific Magazine* December 7, 2008):

> With the Marshall Islands nuclear claims fund down to its last dollars, President Litokwa Tomeing is proposing to use United States grant funds to provide partial payment to nuclear test victims in this western Pacific nation … But the fund that once stood at $150 million is now down to a quarter of a million dollars—barely enough to keep the Tribunal operational for a few more months, said Tribunal Chairman Gregory Danz…

The Tribunal was established in the late 1980s by a

Compact of Free Association between the US and the Marshall Islands with the mandate to adjudicate and compensate personal injury and other claims arising from the 67 American nuclear tests at Bikini and Enewetak. The Tribunal began paying out awards in the early 1990s. It was originally provided about $45 million to compensate both personal injury and land damage claims.

After a multi-year process of hearings, land appraisals and expert testimony, the Tribunal awarded Enewetak, Bikini and Rongelap, the atoll dusted with high-level fallout from the 1954 Bravo test, more than $2 billion in land damage and clean up funding. Only $3.9 million of the land damage claims have been paid due to the lack of funds.

Danz said no existing awards would be paid this year and new awards would be limited to five percent of the total award due to the nearly exhausted compensation fund. The Nuclear claims fund is almost empty, Danz said. As of early November, only $250,916.79 remained.

With total personal injury awards in excess of $96 million, an annual payment of even one-fourth of one percent to each awardee would exhaust the Fund, force the closure of the Tribunal, and foreclose the possibility of any award of payment for future claimants.

Nearly half of the 2,000 islanders who've been awarded nuclear test compensation from the Tribunal have died without receiving 100 percent of their awards, according to Tribunal officials.

On December 12, 2008, AFP reported that the USA refused a request by the Marshall Islands to use grant money to compensate victims of the American nuclear weapons testing program in the western Pacific atoll nation.

"... The $150 million the United States provided for paying settlements ran out three years ago and the US State Department has said there is no obligation to pay more ... More than $22 million remains unpaid for personal injury awards and about two billion dollars is outstanding for land damage awards made by the tribunal."

Then on January 30, 2009, AFP reported:

"A panel of US appeal judges Friday dismissed a claim to enforce a billion-dollar compensation settlement for islanders from two former Pacific nuclear test sites, an attorney for the islanders said. But the attorney said the ruling didn't exonerate the US government for removing the residents of Bikini and Enewetak from their homes and leaving their atolls uninhabitable after the weapons tests. A three-member panel of judges upheld a lower court ruling which dismissed claims filed in 2006 by the people of Bikini and Enewetak in the Marshall Islands, a former US territory in the Western Pacific..."

Pressure on the US government eventually came from the Marshall Islands government after recent elections when Senator Tony deBrum became the Foreign Minister of RMI, as well as from activists world-wide, and from religious leaders.

However, in opposing the will of sole superpower, Senator deBrum became undesirable in his own government. On

February 27, 2009, People's Daily Online reported:

"Marshall Islands Foreign Minister Tony deBrum was sacked from the island nation's cabinet, three weeks after he publicly criticized the administration of President Litokwa Tomeing, Micronesia's Marianas .... In parliament, deBrum criticized the president for not working closely with landowners who are seeking higher rent payments from the US Army that operates the Reagan Test Site missile base at Kwajalein Atoll."

Tad Friend wrote in his article' Lost at Sea' for *Outside Magazine* in March 1997:

Tragic are the people of the lovely Marshall Islands. When America exploded the A-bomb it took their homes, and when it gave comfort it took their ambition, and when it offered only craven solutions it took their hope.

Almost no one wants to remember now one of the most memorable statements of Henry Kissinger (who never ceases to impress people all over the world with his straightforwardness and honesty). Kissinger is quoted in 1969 as saying of the Marshall Islands: "There are only 90,000 people out there. Who gives a damn?"

Back to the present and to the main atoll of Marshall Islands—Majuro—where Jack Niedenthal, Trust Liaison Officer for the People of Bikini Atoll (hired by the Bikinians) has to juggle two allegiances. Born in Harrisburg, Pennsylvania, Mr. Niedenthal has dual citizenship of the USA and the Marshall Islands, holding several high positions, sometimes concurrently, in his adopted country. These include that of the President of Chamber of Commerce and the Chairman of the Board for the Marshall Islands Social Security Administration [MISSA]. The Bikini Island Liaison Office where we meet is decorated with children's eerie drawings of the nuclear explosions.

"The situation is very simple," explains Mr. Niedenthal. "The US came here. It detonated its weapons. All we are demanding is that Bikini be left in the same state as it was before. What I suggest is: clean the place to the paint. And don't expect all 3,900 Bikinians to jump on a boat and go home immediately. But they should be given the choice."

Staff of the *Marshall Islands Journal*, a local weekly tabloid, likes to joke about its own product, even selling T-shirts describing it as the worst newspaper in the world. It is often described as a 'one man show', but its editor and main writer, Giff Johnson, is arguably one of the most important writers in the Pacific, making heroic efforts to keep this tiny and battered nation detectable on the world media map. He does not hide his sympathy which generally lies with the United States, and his dislike of the efforts being made in this part of the world by Chinese competitors for Western interests. His reporting may sometimes be biased, leaning towards the right, but it is mostly indispensable, informative, and factual. As always, nothing is simple in this part of the world. According to Espen Ronnenberg, Giff Johnson's history in the Marshall Islands is long and tragic: he was married to a Bikini Island activist who died of radiation, becoming a national symbol of the fight for compensation.

The *Marshall Islands Journal* is a galaxy away from 'progressive' or left wing publications, but its premises could be easily mistaken for those of some semi-legal left-wing magazine in 1970s Latin America. My meeting with Giff Johnson took place in the rustic editorial room located right above antique printing machines:

"The United States is working on the exit strategy from donor aid," Giff explained. "The US is trying to set up a trust fund. This country has many issues that require immediate solutions; compensation is not the only one. Let's face it, Marshallese see America as the most powerful country on earth, as well as the country that puts money on the table. Part of the grand plan was that Micronesia would never want to be fully independent. And the plan was successful. Look at it now: 70% of the money RMI lives on still comes from the US and Taiwan, of which 60% is from the US, 4 atolls are getting payments from the United States. There is rent paid for leasing Kwajalein. Checks from the rent and other payments used to be cashed here, but now they are cashed in Oakland, California or elsewhere. Marshallese can migrate to the US Depopulation is a huge problem: one third of the people still live on the outer islands but the number is steadily decreasing. And now, while 52,000 people live in RMI, 25,000 already reside in the United States."

According to Espen Ronneberg, an environmental expert employed by SPREP in Samoa and a citizen of the Marshall Islands, at least 500 Marshallese now live in Arkansas, mainly working on chicken farms; others have settled in Orange Country, California and in Utah, where most of them have converted to the Mormon faith.

Internal migration is evident from visiting near-by atolls like Arno, in ancient times renowned for its own culture and unique 'School of Love' for ladies. Now almost depopulated, Arno remains home to only those who are very old or very young.

Driving around Majuro, the magnitude of the problems facing this archipelago seems overwhelming. Garbage and rotting equipment, some dating to the war era, 'decorate' long coral shores. The country is one of the three in Oceania, the other two being Tuvalu and Kiribati, that due to global warming may become uninhabitable in the very near future. Even now when the tide is high, water rolls over the only road connecting all settlements on the atoll bringing transportation to a standstill, making it basically impossible for any agricultural venture, and floods the houses. Bizarre, often outdated flying machines, including old Boeing 727 cargoes marked as *Malaysia Post*, but mostly those with unmarked fuselages, keep landing and taking off from Majuro airport, shaking carton and plywood shacks not far from the runway, their origin and destination unknown or undisclosed.

What is shocking is the idleness of great numbers of local people, as if there was no hope left and nothing to strive for, as if subsistence living or 'permanent retirement' was all there was on offer.

Churches, many belonging to radical and marginal sects, line the main road, as in so many other places of the Pacific. There is a shocking presence of extreme obesity with the range of related illnesses. There is child prostitution that often occurs right under the noses of the authorities, catering predominantly to the foreign—mainly Asian—fishing crews.

In modern history, the Marshall Islands were never truly independent. The United States took over Micronesia from Japan in some of the bloodiest Pacific campaigns of World War II and then governed the region until 1986 as part of a U.N. trusteeship agreement. Immediately after 'independence,' RMI became subject to an agreement with the United States, the so-called Compact of Independent States.

David B. Cohen, Deputy Assistant Secretary for Insular Affairs, United States Department of the Interior, described the Compact Negotiations before the House Committee on Resources on July 17, 2002: "Under the direction of the Interagency Group on Micronesia, chaired by the Department of State, the President's Personal Representative for Micronesian Status Negotiations negotiated the original Compact with representatives of what would become the RMI and the FSM. As a result of the Compact, these nations are commonly referred to as the 'Freely Associated States' (FAS). The Compact was implemented in 1986. Palau also became a Freely Associated State through a subsequent Compact of Free Association, but I will use the term FAS to refer only to the original Freely Associated States of the RMI and the FSM".

But what is hidden behind these technicalities? What is the reality of the Compact? In exchange for cash assistance, the US reserves the right to use FSM, RMI and Palau as its military bases, at all times and for any type of weapons, even nuclear, claiming that it is already paid for.

Cash that flows to RMI and the other countries that signed the Compact has many strings attached, among them political obedience, a by-product of which is the cultural dependency evident in the education sector: "The current state of the education system in the Marshall Islands is one of heavy dependency on the US both for substance (content) and resources (mostly financial), thus there is a lack of ownership amongst Marshallese. Since independence, there have been some efforts to take ownership of the system but so far it has failed. For instance we have been using US textbooks while they have nothing to do with our curriculum," explained Biram Stege, Secretary of Education.

"The issue of Kwajalein can't be separated from the nuclear issue of the past," Senator deBrum told me during our meeting in the restaurant on the second floor of RMI Hotel in Majuro. "Both issues are military and they involve displacement of people, as well as an extremely uncomfortable social situation. It is also an issue of the US abandoning its commitments. In the case of Kwajalein, the United States are claiming that they have the right to use the island for a period much longer than our people agreed to (2016), because they reached an agreement without the RMI government. But our government has no right to allow the use of Kwajalein beyond 2016. And we have no assurances that the United States would treat the people of Kwajalein any differently from how they have treated people of other atolls that they destroyed."

"Even now," continued Senator deBrum, "The US should be engaged in an exit strategy, for lack of better words. We have to know what will be left after they leave. What will be required? What kind of clean-up, replanting, resettlement must be planned? Now we are in 2008—there are only 8 years left. We have to start planting breadfruit trees, coconut palms, other food trees and all that requires time as it takes years before they can be harvested. We have to plant for the future of Kwajalein and the future should not be military. There are many alternatives, such as scientific research using existing installations, fishing, or tourism. So if there is going to be an exit of the United States in 2016, preparations have to be made right now. If not, we should be told now how are they going to remain without our agreement."

"The people of Kwajalein Atoll are confined to a small island. The largest atoll in the world belongs to them, but they are now surviving on slightly more than 56 acres of livable land. There is not much they can do for a living. The lease that is paid to them is the same as it was in 1986 and in reality it is much less now, as it has to support many more people. Ebeye near Kwajalein base is the most overcrowded island in Micronesia. Its social problems are the direct result of the existence of Kwaj."

Many people told me that it would be impossible to comprehend the plight of the Marshallese people as well as those of the entire Oceania, without visiting both Ebeye Island and Kwajalein base on the largest atoll in the world. I decided to go, but before embarking on that journey, I spoke with Paramount Chief Mike Kabua, another Senator representing Kwajalein. Ironically Mike Kabua comes from arguably the most prominent political family in Marshall Islands. His older brother Imata Kabua served as President of the country in 1997-2000, while Amata Kabua was the first President of RMI, serving five consecutive terms between 1979 and 1996.

Next day I was leaving for Kwajalein, and Senator Kabua was kind enough to offer me his people as guides and sponsors for entering the island of Ebeye.

"My God," he exclaimed: "You will soon see such enormous contrasts. I sometimes think that Kwajalein should get independence. We are like a big boat with a small engine. No matter how hard we try, our people are not getting any better. The US presence does not help. They erected security fences and built security posts. We are not used to fences. We are not used to being checked all the time. They say "we are military—that's what we are." But that's not what we are! Now there are Marshallese people serving in their military— even fighting in Iraq. We read, we listen to what is going on in the Middle East and we ask: Why? Iraq is not getting any better—it is getting worse. People are dying every day. And we are sending dozens of Marshallese boys there! One was even shot and injured. The US military pays them, they come to recruit here."

I asked Senator Kabua what exactly the role is of the Paramount Chief in Kwajalein.

"It is to oversee unity of people, land issues and lifestyle," he replied. "In our culture we share everything."

On October 2007, I looked from a window of a Boeing 737 approaching Kwajalein Atoll, pulled out my camera and began snapping photos of the enormous bay which serves as a missile catchment area for the American Star Wars program. Officially, Kwajalein is still part of the Republic of the Marshall Islands (RMI), but its largest island with the same name is leased to the United States. The only airport of the atoll is part of the base and apart from a sporadic and arduous voyage by a cargo vessel the only way for the citizens of RMI to commute between Majuro, where the capital of the country is located, and Kwajalein is by the USA airline Continental Micronesia.

What is evident from the start is that 'Kwaj', as it is known in both the US and RMI, island is rimmed by rotting metal hulks (whatever they are), dotted with huge radar installations, and other concrete Cold-war style buildings looking utterly out of place on this stunning tropical island.

After landing, I walked to the US military checkpoint, my hand luggage left on the floor. A dog sniffed at it; a policewoman explained security regulations; outrageous military propaganda posters decorated the walls. The small immigration checkpoint of the Marshall Islands was stuck in a corner of the room. I had a hard time explaining that I was actually traveling to Ebeye, a small island 4 miles away, a place that provides cheap labor to the American military base, a place of misery—an over-populated and desperate byway of the Marshall Islands, partially inhabited by people from the atolls that fell victim to the American nuclear tests.

To travel from Majuro to Kwajalein Atoll, or, more precisely, to the parts of it that are outside the American base, is truly Kafkaesque. You take an American passenger plane, land on the American military airport, go through the American checkpoint, convince the officer that you are not planning to stay on the base, and only then go through the Marshall Islands checkpoint. After that, the American military (or military looking) staff usher you to the van parked in front of the tiny terminal. You are driven through the entire base with its manicured lawns, tidy buildings, sports and recreation facilities, even a cultural center. At the end, you arrive at the port, where you have to go, once again, through a checkpoint, explaining what brings you to this atoll and whether someone is sponsoring your journey there, and your luggage will be X-rayed. Unless you have someone waiting for you with a private or official boat, you wait for the floating motorized pontoon platform which serves as a shuttle for the workers living on Ebeye and working on the American base on Kwajalein. I was fortunate to have people from the local government waiting for me in the port, as they had been informed about my arrival by Senator deBrum and Paramount Chief Michael Kabua.

The short ride across the sea to Ebeye Island on the government boat was extremely revealing, showing the magnitude of the American military presence in the Marshall Islands—its docks, navy installations and massive concrete structures. Along the shore one could see several well-manicured parks and pathways with benches for the contractors and their families permanently based here. On a lazy afternoon, Kwajalein could feel like a hybrid of some 1980s spy movie and a low-end beach resort in the Caribbean. What is really happening on Kwaj? Long-range missiles are tested. Launched from California's Vandenberg Air Force Base, they fly over 6,000 miles, and then are shot down by interceptors based on Meck Island. Some missiles are simply allowed to fall into the bay, the enormous atoll lagoon the target. That's the theory. That's what is written in encyclopedias and confirmed by local eyewitnesses.

That is what the local government and local citizens who are observing war games from their own backyards, say. But that's not what the US say. After publishing a short report at *Foreign Policy in Focus*, I received an email communication from a certain Mr. Richard Lehner (no title and no organization was indicated). On top of the email was stated 'Classification: UNCLASSIFIED' and 'Caveats: NONE'.

The text followed:

> ... you have taken the Kwajalein missile launch information and mistakenly applied it to the missile defense program. Space X is not part of the missile defense (as you call Star Wars) program as it is a private industry launch system. The Air Force missile launch you cite is also not a part of the missile defense program: it is what is called follow-on testing of intercontinental ballistic missiles (offensive) operated by the Air Force. In these follow-on tests, no interceptor missiles are launched, just the one ICBM from California to Kwajalein.
>
> Also, your sources are wrong about the interceptor missiles. The only interceptors that have been there are the ones that have been used in missile defense

tests beginning in 1999 and concluding in 2005. It only consisted of a single interceptor missile at a time for each individual test and there have never been interceptors based there, and there aren't any now. The US currently has a total of 21 land-based long-range interceptor missiles based in Alaska and three in California. The missile defense test program was moved from Kwajalein in 2005 and now all tests take place in the Pacific Test Range off Hawaii and between Alaska and California.

These comments are printed in order to allow American Intelligence to have its say. The author and several colleagues attempted, but at the end patently failed, to understand the significance of these sublime details.

As reported by *Pacnews* on June 30th, 2009:

> The US Air Force successfully launched an Intercontinental Ballistic Missile (ICBM) Minuteman III early Monday from a California base which reached its target in the Marshall Islands, reports AHN... The missile was fired at 3:01 am from Vandenberg Air Base to test its reliability and accuracy. It was configured with a National Nuclear Security Administration test assembly. The Minuteman III carried three unarmed re-entry vehicles to targets 4,190 miles away, near the Kwajalein Atoll in the Marshall Islands, at speeds of more than 24,000 miles per hour...

Driving and walking through the chain of islets around Ebeye, from South Loi to Gugeegue, and talking to local residents, the author was told again and again that the visible island of Karlos was US owned and held radar installations; that Meck Island was equipped with the launcher for Star Wars missile interceptors; and that interceptors were periodically fired—missiles were intercepted and fell into the lagoon of this enormous atoll, producing dramatic star wars effects, especially on clear starry nights.

After signing the Compact with the US, the Marshall Islands became fully dependent on aid. There is still plenty of bitterness on Kwajalein. Its people believe that they were sacrificed so the rest of the nation could 'enjoy' its cozy dependency on the superpower. It is probably why Senator Mike Kabua spoke about independence. In the meantime, the culture of dependency on the United States has produced at least one wasted generation in both Kwajalein and Majuro.

After an introductory tour of the island, I was left alone, free to explore what appears to be one of the most desperate parts of Oceania.

Just a stone's throw from the super high-tech military base the people of Ebeye have no running water. They experience blackouts. Their traditional diet has almost entirely disappeared, replaced by Spam, corned beef, bacon, and junk food almost exclusively imported from the United States. A great number of inhabitants have diabetes. Preventive medicine is almost unknown and even those who are diagnosed with diabetic conditions continue with their previous lifestyle and diet. As a result, the number of amputees is shocking. Some of them, on wheelchairs, are still munching on sugary ice cream and other types of food, which turn their treatable condition into a deadly disease.

Ebeye is more crowded than Hong Kong and the island is dotted with garbage dumps and pitiful carton shacks, not unlike those in some neighborhoods of Jakarta, one of the most polluted and desperate cities in Asia. Garbage dumps are enormous, with children playing in them or working as scavengers.

One form of American 'foreign assistance' is to dump old and semi-decomposed equipment at Ebeye. There, terrible looking trucks without hoods are left rotting in the center of the island; others, of enormous size and belching black smoke, serve as garbage-collecting vehicles, adding more to the destruction of the environment.

Traditional pastimes have almost entirely disappeared and television sets now beam military programs from Kwajalein base. As mentioned by Senator Mike Kabua, many Marshallese joined the US army and were sent to Iraq to fight. Was it primarily out of desperation or simply from boredom? Or under the influence of the propaganda from the military TV channel? On December 4th, 2008, the Marshall Islands registered its first casualty in the Iraq War—Staff Sgt. Solomon T. Sam, 31, died of wounds from an improvised explosive device in Mosul.

The American military pays rent, but the money goes

directly to the landowners, some of whom have become extremely rich and moved to the United States. While a few Marshallese enjoy the high life, the vast majority live in desperate conditions. Many of those who remember the Japanese occupation claim that even then life was easier and had more dignity than during this 'American era.'

Nobody knows how many people live on Ebeye. Ten years ago it was close to 10,000. Now the estimates are of 13,000, even 15,000. Most jobs are at the US base. At the time of my visit, the local government was only able to employ 107 people with a starting salary of $3 an hour. Even on the base, starting wages are only $4.5–$5 an hour with no benefits provided, and as the budget for the base is decreasing, people are being laid off.

"The majority of our people would never be able to get a job at Kwaj base," explains Aeto Bantol, a government employee. "Even the landowners don't always get jobs. It is not an easy coexistence. Those who live in Ebeye have to search for work on Kwaj. They also have to travel there whenever they want to go anywhere in the Marshall Islands, as the airport is located on the base. The US has some humanitarian funds for our people. They remodeled our government building, for instance, but they are very particular about what projects they get involved in. Some Americans, mainly bachelors, come to Ebeye. They go to bars, some have girlfriends, and others even get married. But overall, there is not much interaction."

"The local government is not very fortunate in getting what is needed here," he continues. "The national government gets what it needs, but not us. Majuro is running everything. It often feels that we have been sidelined."

I talked to regular folk and government people, to Philippine migrant workers and to the children of Ebeye.

Taking more than 1,000 images, I did as much as I could to document the plight of this desperate island.

On the speedboat back to Kwajalein I felt sick to my stomach. I hadn't slept for almost 3 nights as my A/C broke down during the first night and my bed was invaded by a combat platoon of suspiciously corpulent cockroaches. There was no water and no towels in my hotel—supposedly the best on the island. The carpet was stained with betel nut juice, or was it blood? Still, I was fortunate. I had cash. Since no tourists bother to come to Ebeye, the only diner had miserable, but at least semi-hygienic, food. Every morning, a dilapidated local government truck came to pick me up and take me around. I had arrived here by my own choice and my equipment bag had Continental Micronesia tickets to Guam and from there to Tokyo. Therefore I had no right to complain. Compared to everyone else here I was a lucky guy!

For the day of departure I was told to present myself at the checkpoint at least 4 hours before my flight. I took the speed ferry to Kwajalein, went through security, was picked up by the American police (or army or whatever it was) and escorted through the military base to the airport. I then learned that the plane was several hours late:

"It hasn't even left Honolulu yet." Fine, I said: take me to a restaurant. "Oh no," the clerk replied. "You can't stay on the base. You have to get off the island!"

Frazzled, I replied that I am an American citizen and that this is American territory. Outraged I added that this base is where I am going to wait for my plane. But she was unyielding.

"Do you mean that I have to go abroad?" I asked at the end, sarcastically. She only nodded, a grave expression on her face.

"If that's how you look at it …" she said.

People waiting behind me in line were silent and resigned. Back to the police car, back to the checkpoint, to the ferry, to the Marshall Islands.

And then it hit me: nobody complained. Weren't Americans known, even famous, for complaining loudly? Weren't we complaining, just a decade ago, about nearly everything? Weren't we raising hell when the plane was late or when the flight was overbooked? Not any more. Passengers stranded at the airport were smiling servile, submissive smiles.

Then this subversive line of thought took me even further. 'Our military sodomized the entire nation, nuked its people, relocated hundreds, turned the rest into submissive and dependant beings. Then it converted the biggest and one of the most beautiful atolls in the world into missile catchments, into an episode of some bizarre star wars saga. And nobody has read a single word about it! Nobody makes Borat-style films about the situation in Kwaj and Ebeye.'

While the private contractors and military with their families enjoy the 'cultural center' and craft shop on the base, while they play golf next to the runway, while their children have cute little playgrounds and beaches and benches to watch the sunset from, the people of the Marshall Islands are crammed like sardines on polluted and dirty Ebeye and elsewhere around the Kwaj Atoll, their feet and legs amputated because they can't get adequate food and treatment for their medical conditions as well as a decent education!

And while I was at it, I continued with this dangerous reasoning:

'So what happened to our journalist traditions? Weren't many of our best novelists also brilliant journalists? Didn't fiction and nonfiction go hand in hand, complementing each other, inspiring each other? Where are our novelists? Why don't they write about the Marshall Islands and Ebeye? Why don't they write in the mass media?'

At that point I began to worry about myself.

'These thoughts are probably the result of dehydration and an acute lack of sleep,' I thought. 'Nobody asks such stupid questions in this day and age. Of course nobody writes about Kwaj and Ebeye. And of course no major publication will invite me or will allow me to write about this place. Because they are all disciplined, good and obedient boys and girls. Because there is almost no independent journalism left in my country. Editors are corporate guys.'

I wandered around Ebeye, mad and tired, desperate. Five hours later I took the speedboat back to Kwaj, went through security, and was escorted to the airport again. Then, together with several other passengers I was locked in some hangar called a waiting room. Continental Micronesia didn't provide food or even water. There was no explanation and no apology. Once again we removed our belts and shoes while going through security.

"Can I keep on my underwear?" I asked.

"Sir?!"

I heard the cold military bark.

When the plane finally arrived, I was still seven hours away from Guam. This was the famous 'island hopper', stopping at all the airports of the Federated States of Micronesia that are on the way: Kozurai, Phonopei, Chuuk. FSM being yet another 'Compact' country where the local people have to travel on the US carrier when they want to go from the outer islands to the capital. I realized I would have only 3 hours of sleep before catching my Tokyo bound flight early in the morning.

To my surprise, the other passengers welcomed the arrival of the plane with loud cheers. No resistance, no revolution in the making, no sarcasm. They reminded me of North Koreans welcoming the Dear Leader. Then I realized I had had enough. I suddenly yelled at my fellow passengers:

"Why are you grinning like hyenas? Aren't you pissed off? Aren't we going to demand an explanation or compensation? Anything?!"

There was dead silence. People were staring at me in horror. A security guard slowly approached. He was twice my size.

"Do you have a problem?" he asked in a chilling voice.

"Yes," I said. "My plane is almost six hours late. I was kicked out, sent abroad to wait for it. I am hungry, thirsty and pissed off. And everybody looks like I deserve to be taken to Guantanamo Bay for saying it!"

People watched me as if I were a suicide bomber. Some began moving away, bracing for a blast.

I realized I had said something that was not supposed to be pronounced. Guantanamo Bay! After all, I was on an American military base. Yes. Would Joseph Heller now be declared a terrorist for writing about the bombing of his own airport in Catch-22? Would others be locked in secret prisons in the Middle East or Eastern Europe for writing books that justify the struggle for justice? The real struggle for justice, not the dominant media lie. Can one end up in a concentration camp these days, or lose citizenship, for speaking out about our military bases? Can one be put away for declaring that we are taking advantage of defenseless people and that our star wars technologies are just expensive, immoral and destructive toys for private contractors and top military brass?

Is one still allowed to scream, to protest—to ridicule insanity? I looked at the guard and then at the passengers.

I used to love America for its spirit of rebelliousness. Now I saw servility and compliance.

I was in the middle of an American high security military installation, surrounded by passengers who were, at least many of them, private contractors working on the base. I was at least risking being denied boarding. But I couldn't do otherwise.

"And I have another problem," I said. "I have a problem with this base, which should be closed down and returned to the people of Kwajalein."

And then … nothing! The security guard said nothing. The door finally opened, and Continental Micronesia staff invited us to board the plane. I was not arrested; nobody put a bullet through my brain. I boarded the plane and took off. That simple.

Later I saw the enormous beauty of Kwajalein Atoll below the wing and my glasses became foggy and for some reason I had to swallow very hard and turn my face away from the window.

The great Tongan writer Epeli Hau'ofa once wrote:

"As far as I am concerned, anyone who has lived in our region and is committed to Oceania is an Oceanian."

I lived and worked in this part of the world for years. Its suffering deeply moved me. It was, therefore, my responsibility and duty to attempt to describe the plight of the people in this part of the world. Nowhere in the Pacific is this plight so urgent and injustice so outrageous as in the Marshall Islands. And nowhere is neocolonial contempt towards the local population and its culture so open and evident as here.

In Guam, in the arrival hall, several photos of young Pacific Islanders —those who had recently died in Iraq— welcomed me.

The Scarred Beauty And Unfulfilled Hopes of Port Moresby

THE ROYAL PAPUA YACHT CLUB WOULD NOT FEEL OUT OF place in any wealthy Australian or New Zealand city. On seemingly endless outdoor terraces overlooking elegant sailboats and the Moresby Harbor, expatriates gather for cold beer and exchange the latest stories and political gossip. Laptop computers are connected through the fast wireless network; slot machines in a gambling room swallow and regurgitate coins with silkworm speed and happy sounds. Private yachts elegantly float on clean water. This speck of land could be in some tropical paradise in the Caribbean or French Polynesia. But it is not: it is right in the midst of the city which periodically hits headlines as 'The least livable capital on earth'.

Not far away from the bay, an impressive six-lane highway climbs then cuts through the mountain connecting the center of Port Moresby with Waigani, the government district. The sun is reflected from the glass and steel of elegant high-rises. Black smoke from ruined mufflers spoil the breathtaking vista, but the road is the most modern anywhere in Oceania.

Viewed from the terraces of the Royal Papua Yacht Club, Port Moresby appears to be serene and wealthy, the proud capital of Papua New Guinea, a nation of well over 6 million people, countless islands, abundant natural resources and an estimated 867 languages. It certainly appears better off and wealthier than the cities across the border—in oppressed West Papua ruled from Jakarta.

But not far from the club, on the highest floors of the Crown Plaza Hotel Executive lounge, the Australian military, always ready to 'assist' in this part of the world, gathers to discuss the security situation in the country. And the United Nations prepares to impose security phase 2 for its personnel—the same level as in war-torn Afghanistan.

Ten kilometers from the center, 'Mile 6 Settlement' offers a sobering alternative to the idyllic vistas depicted on the colorful postcards on sale in the gift shops of expensive hotels. Here, the walls of dirt-poor dwellings consist of rusty metal sheets. Thousands of families live in metal or cardboard shacks with no access to clean drinking water. Although there are no official statistics available, the crime rate in Mile 6 Settlement is one of the highest in the world.

According to residents, only a handful of families can afford to send their children to school and the great majority of men and women lack permanent jobs. Hundreds of settlement dwellers hang out aimlessly at the sides of unpaved roads, staring into the distance, playing cards, and boozing or chewing betel nut.

But Mile 6 Settlement is not the only part of the city where misery concentrates. There is also 9 Mile Settlement and several other 'miles' known only by their numbers— their names come from the old administration practice of identifying areas according to their distance from the GPO (General Post Office).

The Anglican Church of Papua New Guinea describes 9 Mile Settlement in pragmatic language:

> Nine Mile is one of the most violent and trouble-ridden settlements in the city. It has a mixed population, with large numbers of unemployed young people. Alcohol and drug abuse (marijuana is cheap, easily grown or bought and is also a lucrative income earner for many) are rife. There is much violence, especially on pay fortnights.
>
> Here, as elsewhere in the poor parts of Port Moresby and the rest of Papua New Guinea (PNG), sexually transmitted diseases, and HIV/AIDS in particular, are growing at an alarming rate.

Mary Jonduo, a community worker in Port Moresby, who specializes in literacy and non-formal education, explains: "It is really frightening how quickly HIV is spreading across the country. As you know, our land is mountainous and composed of many outer islands, and it is hard to know exactly how many of us live in PNG, even in Port Moresby. This means that we do not have an exact count of infections. Besides, there is a stigma associated with the disease so even if some people know that they are infected; they will not go for testing. Last year there was a case of an HIV infected person buried alive in a village in the Highlands. Instead of helping people who are suffering, we end up disappearing them."

"For the past few years the spread has been incredibly fast," continues Mr. Jonduo. "The principal reason, I believe, is the state of literacy in our country. Our literacy rate from the 2000 Census is around 56 percent, but in fact I think it is much lower in many parts of the country since it is based on self-declaration. We are talking about almost half of the population who cannot read or write or understand a simple sentence in a language. This in itself is a national catastrophe, even before talking about HIV. Another problem is corruption. With the millions of dollars we receive per year for prevention, care and support, politicians regularly hold 'seminars', 'conferences' and 'workshops' at very expensive hotels. The people who really need support are never invited nor know how the support intended for them is being spent. Corruption and nepotism is everywhere in PNG."

One of the largest and oldest villages on the outskirts of the city is called Hanuabada. It is built over the sea on stilts, in order to prevent damage from flooding by changing tides. With more than a hundred years of history, at first sight, Hanuabada—the 'Great Village' in local language—looks similar to some stilt dwellings that became tourist attractions in Southeast Asia, such as Kampong Ayer in Brunei or traditional water villages in Kalimantan/Borneo and Thailand.

However, in PNG, it is a microcosm of countless problems this country has to face. Evidence of poverty is everywhere, from the lack of sanitation to the lack of shoes on the feet of many children, as well as the adults. When the tide is low, the seabed is hardly visible through the thick smelly layer of garbage that is never cleaned up.

Several makeshift barricades block our car as we approach Hanuabada and groups of angry villagers can be spotted at almost every corner. My local colleague explains that just two days earlier, the intoxicated son of one of the MPs ran over and killed two children from Hanuabada, and the village exploded in spontaneous outrage. Riots devastated several dwellings and services along the main road.

As elsewhere in and around the capital city, racial and communal tension is reaching boiling point, while trust in politicians has long faded.

Mr. Araka, a local community leader, explains: "In the Port Moresby area, there are 250,000 migrants and only 30,000 native Motu people. The entire capital area is developed on Motu land and the natives are being pushed to the edges of the city. They have lost almost everything and emotions are running high."

Xenophobia and racial tensions are among the main problems of the city and the country. My friend Walter, a Ministry of Education employee, died from a heart attack during my visit. Still in his fifties, he had been beaten twice by local gangs and was left unconscious on the street. Because he had exceptionally black skin, the thugs thought he was from Bougainville, a province with a strong independence movement. Fighting between ethnic groups with more than 800 languages and cultures is tearing the country apart.

Most of the settlements consist of economic migrants from the highlands, escaping the harsh life of subsistence farming, hoping that Port Moresby will fulfill their dreams of well paid jobs and excitement. Unfortunately, as in the capitals of many poor countries all over the world, only a small fraction of the migrants manage to find any kind of regular work, leaving the rest to make ends meet by relying on seasonal work. Some turn to crime and prostitution in order to survive.

To make matters worse, Port Moresby in particular and PNG in general is facing a large influx of 'external refugees'— from the half of the island occupied by Indonesia. One of the oldest settlements around Port Moresby, 8 Mile Settlement consists of political and economic refugees from neighboring Papua, where conditions are even worse.

Political repression and religious discrimination, and indiscriminate mining and logging by Indonesian and foreign companies are among the reasons for the continuous flow of refugees across the border. Earlier migration policies of Jakarta, not unlike those of the Soviet Union in the Baltic Republics, were aimed at making the locals a minority in their own land. These policies are partially to blame for the deepening conflict in Papua, formerly known as Irian Jaya. Papuans are predominantly dark-skinned Melanesians, like those across the border in Papua New Guinea and Australian Aborigines. Many are animists or Christians or both. Immigrants from Java and Sumatra are predominantly Muslim and generally contemptuous towards the locals.

John Pilger wrote in his powerful article 'Secret war against defenseless West Papua:

> Indonesia's brutal occupation of West Papua, a vast, resource-rich province—stolen from its people, like East Timor—is one of the great secrets of our time.
>
> An estimated 100,000 Papuans, or 10 per cent of the population, have been killed by the Indonesian military. This is a fraction of the true figure, according to refugees. In January 2006, 43 West Papuans reached

Australia's north coast after a hazardous six-week journey in a dugout. They had no food, and had dribbled their last fresh water into their children's mouths.

"We knew," said Herman Wainggai, the leader, "that if the Indonesian military had caught us, most of us would have died. They treat West Papuans like animals. They kill us like animals. They have created militias and jihadis to do just that. It is the same as East Timor."

In its report published on July 17th, 2008, The Economist claimed:

...that the Indonesian government has discontinued its programme of transportation to Papua and elsewhere to relieve overcrowding on Java. But migrants are still flooding in. Official figures show that in 2004 Muslims were 23% of the region's 2 million plus population. In reality the proportion of Muslims is thought to be much higher, probably over half now, but the government has not published updated figures.

Intimidation of non-Muslims in Papua is common. Outright racist treatment of natives by government and military officials is well documented, although the Indonesian media is only allowed to see what the authorities allow them to see, and foreign media are rarely, if ever, granted visas to enter the province.

The Free Papua Movement (OPM), which is illegal as is any movement anywhere in Indonesia that calls for self-determination, is still active in many parts of the territory. The brutality of the armed forces is epic, triggering new waves of native refugees to neighboring PNG. It is believed that at least 120,000 Papuans have already lost their lives during the Jakarta colonial rule, in what, as in the case of East Timor, could be described as genocide. Amnesty International believes that Papua has lost approximately one sixth of its population, over 100,000 people, as a result of the occupation.

In October 2004, the then Director of Education of PNG, Sir Peter Baki, explained to me the plight of many Papuan children in the occupied territory: "Our inspectors who work with the children were repeatedly told that: Indonesian troops come regularly to remote villages in Papua. When they see girls they like, they detain them. Families are sent away and the soldiers hold the girls until they have forced them to have sex with them. Then the girls are told to remain silent; otherwise the army would destroy their whole village. It's that simple: if the girls try to press charges and identify soldiers who raped them, relatives would be killed and the entire village could be destroyed... There are two refugee camps near the border; one of them is called Awian. There are plenty of children there, who came from the other side. We irregularly send officers from the Ministry of Education there to see what can be done. We are encouraging children to go and attend Monfort School there."

Children are not the only ones who are escaping brutality, nor are the recent refugees the only ones to inhabit settlements around Port Moresby. Mile 8 Settlement is full of men and women with bitter memories and terrifying stories from the past. Several former leaders from Papua speak reluctantly about pre-1974 actions of Jakarta: kidnapping of important Papuan figures, flying them to Java where Jakarta authorities either tortured or attempted to bribe them, pushing them to vote for joining Indonesia.

Harlene Joku, star reporter at The National, the daily newspaper in Port Moresby, who is originally from Papua, summarized her feelings: "My father was put through torture there. Indonesian officials in Port Moresby are now very nice to me: they invite me to go back, at least to visit. And I am honest to them: I can't go; I will not. But my heart is there."

The Indonesian Embassy in Port Moresby is extremely active. There are accusations that it is attempting to increase its influence over PNG, often bribing officials. Generally, PNG is petrified by the huge and brutal (towards its minorities) country across its borders. Now even the lot of long-term refugees on PNG soil is becoming uncertain. Recently, the Australia West Papua Association reported:

> News that the 500 West Papuan refugees who had been living at the 8-mile settlement outside Port Moresby for 20 years were facing eviction was broadcast mid-2006. News that more than 214 West Papuan refugees were granted an injunction to stay until February 15, 2007 was reported in December, 2006.

The May 31st, 2007 Vanuatu *Daily Post*:

> West Papuan representative in Vanuatu, Dr Otto Ondawame, reported an incident when Indonesian officials and Kopassus military were escorted to the 8-mile settlement, unannounced, by PNG police. The 8-mile residents chased the 'delegation' out of the settlement.

UNHCR Head in Port Moresby, Ms Wallaya Pura, said she

was aware of Indonesia's efforts to repatriate the refugees, and of their efforts to coerce the PNG government to support this program. Dr Ondawarme similarly claims that the PNG government was working in collaboration with the Indonesian Embassy in PNG and pro-special autonomy groups led by Frans Albert Yoku to force the West Papuans back to Indonesia.

The situation deteriorated to such a level that on July 1st 2008 the Association of West Papuan Refugees produced an appeal for resettlement in a third country.

Port Moresby is encircled by squatter settlements of various levels of desperation. In many of them, tensions are running high. The original inhabitants of the area blame economic migrants from the central part of PNG for taking away their land and work opportunities.

Communal violence is not uncommon and the crime rate in the country in general and the capital city in particular is one of the highest in the world, although exact statistics do not exist.

Authorities in June 2009 razed homes, businesses and banana gardens in the Five Mile settlement following three murders there in a period of just a few days.

Mainly due to crime, Port Moresby is repeatedly rated as the world's least livable city on earth. (In 2006, it shared this dubious distinction with Algiers).

PNG and the neighboring Solomon Islands are often described as 'last frontier' countries which are visited only by a handful of independent travelers. The deteriorating security situation is only one reason keeping foreigners away. Traveling in PNG is extremely expensive; almost everything has to be imported and companies often adopt a 'high-risk, high-return' approach. A return flight to one of the remote areas of the country from the capital may easily cost US$700 or more. In a recent positive development, the government purchased several modern ferries to ease movement between the islands.

Despite its many problems, PNG's assets include its hundreds of unique cultures, breathtaking islands and unspoiled jungle, fauna and flora that can be hardly matched in their diversity by any other country. But now even the flora and fauna are under heavy attack, particularly from international logging and mining companies. (This is further described in the Paradise Lost chapter of this book.)

Considering its size (around 300,000 inhabitants) Port Moresby is culturally vibrant and cosmopolitan, with all ethnic groups from PNG represented here, as well as Caucasians, people from the Sub-Continent and East and Southeast Asia. By Oceania standards, it is a cultural powerhouse and together with Suva, the capital of Fiji, the only 'real' city in the Pacific Island Nations. Crime aside, it is relatively tidy and well organized.

Local media are vibrant and very outspoken, although hardly immune to corruption and to influence from local and foreign business interests, particularly those from Indonesia, Australia and Malaysia.

After the incomparable and splendid Jean-Marie Tjibaou Cultural Centre in New Caledonia, the National Museum is the second most impressive institution of its kind in Melanesia. Although somewhat dilapidated on the outside, it hosts many superb examples of totems, masks and shields, as well as a magnificent outrigger canoe.

Parliament House, an architectural masterpiece, was opened by Prince Charles in 1984. It was built in traditional Sepik-architecture, with mosaics depicting Papua New

Guinean motifs. Huge Sepik masks and splendid butterflies decorate the interior. The Parliament Chamber is famous for its epic—often physical—battles; almost all heavy chairs are now screwed to the floor, as MPs have a tendency to throw them at each other when possessed by political zeal.

Port Moresby has something unheard of in a city of its size in either the Pacific or Southeast Asia: the Moresby Art Theatre (MAT), with periodic performances of well-crafted theatre plays.

In sharp contrast to the sadness of the cities across the border in Indonesia-controlled West Papua, extremely vibrant cultural life and entertainment form the main pillars of the lifestyle of Port Moresby. PNG may be almost as poor as West Papua, it may be corrupt and exploited, but without any doubt it is free. It feels free and it acts free.

Music is everywhere, from the Constable (Police) Band marching through the city center on the weekends to a diverse and exciting club culture. Due to the relatively large number of expatriates based in the city, it is not uncommon to encounter Philippine or Australian stars and starlets performing at the sleek Gold Club, Mustang Sally's or other well established night-spots. Citizens of Port Moresby are determined club-goers. Security concerns are ignored and on the hottest nights, from Wednesday to Saturday, the action rarely starts before 10 p.m., sometimes much later.

The local music scene is extremely strong, with support from the local FM stations. Almost every village has its own string band. A fusion of jazz-rock and indigenous sounds are very popular. PNG has produced world-famous artists, including Sanguma and George Telek.

The contemporary art scene is also vivid, despite the death in 2003 of Mathias Kauage, PNG's internationally acclaimed painter. Paintings, sculptures and masks can be found in several galleries or right on the street, much of it, including dance, song, sculpture and body adornment, being strongly related to local rituals.

Possibly the greatest symbol of PNG classical art is its magnificent masks and totems, displayed in the middle of the major avenues of the city, and decorating the lobbies of all important hotels, banks, offices and government buildings. Some of the best examples of this unique creative expression can be found in the world's great museums, including the Metropolitan Museum of Art in New York and the Musee du Quai Branly in Paris.

Port Moresby and its environs were part of the WWII theatre. The wreck of the cargo ship MV MacDhui in Moresby Harbor, sunk by Japanese planes in the early days of the war, is still clearly visible from the coast of the capital city. Not far from the city is the Kokoda Track—the site of one of the bloodiest battles in the Pacific during WWII, mainly between Australian and Japanese forces—and Bomana War Cemetery, where 4000 Australian and Papua New Guinea WWII soldiers are buried.

PNG gained independence from Australia in 1975 but the citizens of Port Moresby still compare their city to Australian metropolises. Despite the great difference in incomes between Australia and PNG, with half-shut eyes the center of Port Moresby resembles any midsize cities that could be found in the 'rich world'. Its infrastructure and city planning are good.

The south coast along Ela Beach is dotted with elegant villas and condominiums. Ela beach itself is public and free, consisting of seaside promenades and playgrounds for children. Streets of Port Moresby are wide and well maintained, with comfortable sidewalks and well-organized and dedicated areas for parking. Modern buildings are of relatively high quality and the port is spotless and efficient. In many ways, the capital of PNG appears better planned and organized and better maintained than any city in Southeast Asia, with the exception of Singapore and Kuala Lumpur.

But first impressions may be deceiving. Some street corners have been taken over by the 'rascals', street children, often thieves, many of whom have never entered a classroom. Sidewalks are red from spat out betel nut. Betel nuts are legal and mildly narcotic and chewing them is a national pastime in PNG and other Pacific nations. It is not recommended to walk on the streets of Port Moresby after sundown; violent attacks, rape and even murder are common.

After 6 p.m. taxis have two men sitting on the front seats: the driver and a bodyguard. Hundreds of desperate men and women are sitting on the sidewalks, waiting for any kind of work that might come their way. And the settlements encircling the capital speak of the desperate need for change in this fascinating but battered nation.

"The worst violence usually occurs in January and February, the time when the desperate families try to scramble money for school fees for their children," explained Harlyne Joku of *The National* newspaper. "Some adults are literally forced to rob in order to keep their offspring in the classrooms. Although elementary schools are theoretically free, parents are still expected to pay the fee— too steep for the majority."

As stated earlier, the situation can be at least partially blamed on the corruption and incompetence of the PNG government. As a consequence, much more than half of the population is still functionally illiterate.

Attending local schools does not always guarantee a step in the right direction. Recent wars inside and between schools indicate that the situation is out of control. "Police are unable to prevent infighting between students as more and more students are involved … especially students attending upper primary schools, secondary schools, and those in grades 11 and 12," explained a local policeman. On January 8, 2009, *The National* wrote that:

> Port Moresby has been placed among the top five murder capitals in the world, a ranking by a foreign publication that has got Police Commissioner Gari Baki fuming. The Washington DC-based Foreign Policy publication, in its edition last September, lists Port Moresby alongside Caracas (Venezuela), Cape Town (South Africa), New Orleans (USA) and Moscow (Russia) as cities where you have a very good chance of getting murdered.

The five cities appear to have been selected more or less randomly; Caracas' statistics were inflated while several cities all over the world with higher murder rates were not mentioned at all. Despite the shabbiness and clear political motivation of the reporting by Foreign Policy, there is no denying that Port Moresby suffers from extreme problems.

What went wrong? PNG is extremely rich in natural resources. It is one of the world's most stunning countries and if managed well, it could become a great magnet for travelers from all over the world. But as it stands, its GDP per capita is $750 a year, comparable to that of its poor neighbor—Indonesia.

Foreign commercial and political interests as well as corruption and mismanagement in local power structures are mainly to blame for the present situation. The country's vulnerability to exploitation by multi-national companies, especially those involved in mining and logging, is the epic problem, and one that is extremely difficult to solve. Foreign companies take full advantage of the vulnerability of the local population and its culture that is very different from those that are predominantly based on business interests. Foreign governments do little or nothing to restrain companies from their countries when it comes to their often devastating involvement in PNG. One major Malaysian logging company controls an important daily newspaper, airline and, according to local attorneys, several members of the government. If opposed, it doesn't hesitate to kill, beat up and rape people.

Ron Crocombe wrote the following in *South Pacific*:

> Mineral discoveries elsewhere in PNG led to enormous tensions over the allocation of benefits; these tensions caused further deterioration in law and order, and were aggravated by exposure of corruption in high places. Police and judicial systems were unable to punish more than a tiny proportion of offenders, which made crime easy and rewarding, and undermined public confidence in the government and the social system. PNG forces have attempted several coups but none has succeeded, as no ethnic or other section of the population is large or coordinated enough to dominate all others. The government structure is intact, but its functioning has deteriorated.

After independence, PNG suffered from several disasters, including the civil war in Bougainville in which an estimated 20,000 people lost their lives, and from strained relations with its neighbor—Indonesia.

The fact that PNG consists of hundreds of distinct cultures and that its people feel allegiance to their tribes, to so-called 'One Talk' rather than to the country as a whole, doesn't help to govern it as one nation. And those who govern are too embedded in their own clans and personal interests. Since independence, not one government has served its full term, being forced to resign through a no-confidence vote.

This unique nation, consisting of deep traditions, hundreds of cultures and languages, outstanding beauty as well as natural wealth, may be reaching a crossroad. If social explosion erupts, it could lead to long and bloody fighting, to a civil war, which would make any progress impossible for decades to come. But if dedication to progressive social change were to prevail, PNG could emerge as one of the world's most fascinating and diverse nations.

Samoa: One Nation, Two Failed States

To fly from Samoa, formerly Western Samoa, to American Samoa—two utterly remote split-nation island territories in the South Pacific—used to be extremely easy and cheap. One only had to drive 5 kilometers from the capital, Apia, to the small village of Fagalii, to buy the ticket, chat for a while with fellow travelers sitting on plastic bags and outdated suitcases, go through an improvised security and passport control, then board a little propeller-driven aircraft to Pago Pago, capital of American Samoa, a 20 minute hop given favorable winds.

Nowadays, the tiny Twin Otter of Polynesian Airlines takes off from the international airport of Faleolo, at the opposite end of Upolu Island, a 40-minute drive from Apia. It is considered a regular international flight, so to board it one has to face the habitually obnoxious airport and security staff, pay a departure tax, present a boarding pass to the guard, pass through passport control and then through an onerous security check. In contrast, passengers from American Samoa to Samoa do not even face a metal detector. Prices for this short hop have skyrocketed to US$140 for a round trip, a fortune for would-be local 'commuters'. The other option is an overnight trip over generally rough seas, using the small car ferry MV Lady Naomi. This is not a cheap or pleasant alternative.

Immigration procedures are complicated partly because of the diplomatic saga that began in 2005. The Attorney General of American Samoa, Sialaga Malaetasi Togafau, proclaimed that he had tightened immigration rules because the 14-day permit allowing citizens of Samoa to enter the US territory of American Samoa had been abused.

"The issuance of such permits," he said, "would only be granted to those who qualify: business people and persons who need to travel urgently for medical reasons or to attend a funeral."

The Attorney General ordered Samoan authorities to begin pre-scanning permit applicants.

What was not pronounced but was widely understood to lie behind the decision was that at the time, approximately 600 Samoan illegal workers, out of about 1,000, were overstaying in American Samoa. Many of them worked in the two large tuna canneries on the outskirts of Pago Pago.

Samoa is well known across the Pacific for its nationalism and its glorification of its culture; its injured pride led to retaliation. Samoa declared that all visiting American Samoans would need to obtain travel permits and pay an entry fee of between US$10 and US$30, depending on the mood of officials.

Regulations keep changing and are often ambiguous.

The US Department of State defines entry requirements of American Samoans to Samoa as follows:

> US nationals who are not US citizens, and who are resident in American Samoa, must obtain a visitor permit prior to all travel to Samoa. US nationals have not been permitted to travel to Samoa on certificates of identity since May 2005 except on a case-by-case basis. US law distinguishes between individuals who are citizens and those who are nationals. The US passport bio-page indicates whether one is a citizen or a non-citizen national. From March 22, 2006, visitor permits to travel to Samoa can be applied for at the new Samoa Consulate General office in Pago Pago, American Samoa.

American Samoa's Governor Togiola Tulafona has called Samoa's entry certificate a 'revenue-generating permit'. He notes that many Samoan citizens come to American Samoa to earn a living, while very few American Samoans go to Samoa with the intention of staying.

Probably the most embarrassing chapter of the conflict was the case of MV Lady Naomi that arrived in Pago Pago in October 2006, carrying the National University of Samoa rugby team. None of the players had the necessary entry permit. Attorney General Togafau of American Samoa fined the operator of the vessel, Samoan Shipping Corporation, US$20,000, and prevented the young people from disembarking.

The issue of the fine was subsequently settled, mainly on a technicality, since none of the rugby players actually stepped on American Samoa's soil. But the incident indicates just how poisoned the atmosphere between the two Samoas has become. Separated from each other across the ocean by just a few dozen kilometers, inhabitants of the two countries find their ties are increasingly severed. Fragmentation of the Pacific cannot serve the interests of its impoverished inhabitants, but it continues relentlessly.

Independent [formally Western] Samoa, the region's first independent country, having gained independence from New Zealand in 1962, has over 180,000 inhabitants. With US$2,593 GDP per capita it is very poor, yet it has some of the highest prices in the world as almost everything is imported. Among numerous paradoxes is the fact that to boost its pride it provides international organizations with inflated statistics, while fighting a decision by the World Bank that it is ready to 'graduate' Samoa from its Least Developed Country status (LDC).

Most of the long-term economic growth comes from remittances. Although slightly declining in 2007, remittances still represent approximately a quarter of the country's GDP.

As Cherelle Jackson reported in *Island Business* magazine (2007):

> Remittance receipts account for a growing percentage of the country's GDP, according to the World Bank... 41.9 percent of Tonga; 26 percent of Samoa's and 6.7 percent of Fiji's GDP.

"The cash that immigrants send home is a vital source of income for the daily survival of Pacific Islands' households," said Dr Manjula Luthria, a senior economist with the World Bank's Pacific office.

Given the location of two of the world's largest tuna

processing factories that provide relatively high wages in US dollars, American Samoa, an 'unincorporated' US territory with 66,000 inhabitants, is one of the main magnets for economic migrants from Samoa. Its GDP per capita is $9,041 (2005), approximately 3.5 times higher than in Samoa, although well below the US poverty rate.

Migration from Samoa is massive: according to New Zealand government statistics, in 2006, 131,103 people of Samoan ethnicity lived in New Zealand, about half of all those with Pacific ethnicity. Further tens of thousands live in the United States, Australia and elsewhere. Samoa has a 'Samoa Quota Scheme' with the Government of New Zealand whereby up to 1,100 people can legally migrate annually. Moreover, Samoa is one of four countries benefiting from a recently launched seasonal workers scheme. Like many Pacific Island nations, more Samoans live abroad than in their own country.

There are many reasons besides economics for this. Samoa can be an extremely oppressive society where imported but not fully implemented democratic principles vie with the traditional rule of the matais (chiefs). Ordinary citizens are often tightly controlled by these chiefs, and also by the churches.

The country is plagued with land disputes that are tearing apart entire families and clans. "The government took away the land from its own people," recalled Professor Vavao Fetui. "When Samoa became independent, the government took over the land and sold it to the people with a lot of money— then mostly members of parliament. The present big land owners are actually the people from that first government."

Land disputes are a big issue all over Oceania, but in Samoa they reach particularly alarming levels. According to the editor of *Samoa Observer*, followed only by jealousy, land disputes are the main reason for a very high but statistically undocumented crime rate. Land disputes block development, and even some large construction projects from abroad.

"Samoans are very materialistic people," continued Professor Vavao Fetui. "They simply can't look behind materialism."

Suicide rates are very high in both Samoas. Sexual abuse and the rape of children are among the highest in the world, although there are no comprehensive official statistics available. So are domestic violence and violent crimes in general. While the local press reports grizzly cases of murder, it does not publish statistics. This can be due to political reasons or simply because it does not have access to them and is unwilling or incapable of generating them on its own.

"We have no access to police statistics," explained the editor of *Samoa Observer*, Mata'afa Keni Lesa. "The murder rate and other types of crime are extremely high in Samoa, but we are never told exactly how high. We have to rely solely on our own sources. On the other hand, foreigners have designated Samoa for political reasons as some sort of success story in this part of the world, fully ignoring reality. Anyone who takes a stroll even in the downtown area of Apia would have to see reality! Child beggars, miserably poor people everywhere. All you have to do is go to the villages and you will see what is happening. A very small group of our people is rich, even in the cities."

"The rates of rape, child abuse, domestic violence are all very high," continued Mata'afa Keni Lesa, "but when you look at warnings by foreign embassies, they are played down and Samoa is pitched as a generally safe country. This does a great disservice to our people. Let's face it:

supposedly, officially, this is a democracy. But there is so much corruption in Samoa and so little transparency that we can't even put our hands on any statistics. It is really scary!"

A cover story from the *Samoa Observer* on May 8, 2008 is typical:

> A father of nine is in police custody for allegedly kicking his wife's face, killing her, last Friday morning, at Faleu Manono... He was trying to wake up his wife, Elisapeta Lei'atawa, 49, to fetch the milk for their grandchildren. But she said something to him so he kicked her on the jaw ...

Earlier this year, Supreme Justice Patu Tiava'asu'e Falefatu Sapolu allowed a 19 year old babysitter to go free after he confessed that he was playing with the genitals of a 3 year old girl. The judge ruled that, as shown by expert witnesses, the girl was not a virgin anymore at the time she was abused by the babysitter. He therefore set the defendant free. There was no investigation as to who took this child's virginity.

Grizzly reporting like that on the cover pages of local newspapers appears every week. A mother ran over a baby that cried excessively with her 4WD. There are countless rape cases against children, even infants. Young people are killed in fighting between villages.

On January 19, 2009, the Samoa Observer reported:

> Father finds daughter dead. She was naked. There were holes on her legs; it looked like someone stabbed her with a knife... Her face was all bruised and her body was starting to puff up. There were pieces of cloth tied

to her neck and pieces of the shirt she was wearing that day hanging from her neck.

During more than 5 years in Oceania, I repeatedly tried to arrange a meeting with the Police Commissioner and with Supreme Court judges. I wanted comments on the obviously outrageously high crime rate, one that has long been ignored by the main players, the US, Australia and New Zealand, which see Samoa as a staunch ally and free-market champion. Not one meeting was granted, something unthinkable everywhere else in Oceania where access to government officials for reporters, filmmakers and writers is possible and often granted.

At one point, the *Samoa Observer* editor joined me in requesting statistics from Police through the official channels—to no avail. While waiting for the acting Commissioner—who was himself under investigation for alleged sexual abuse—at the brand new, multi-million dollar Police Headquarters built by Australia, I asked several police officials whether Australia made its massive help to Samoan police conditional, whether they requested transparency. The answer was unanimous: no transparency was required and no conditions were attached. Officers had no idea what was I talking about.

And so the Samoan Police got its modern headquarters building and dozens of Australian police cars, which now roam the streets of Apia at excessive speed, creating traffic hazards. Despite the fact that people are allegedly routinely beaten up and tortured in detention, that law enforcement agents allegedly recently sodomized two jailed girls and at least one person has recently died in police custody, the Samoan police enjoy unprecedented support from the major players in the region.

Disciplining children in Samoa would be considered child abuse in most developed and even developing countries: brutality against the weak—mainly girls, boys and women—is epic. Severe beating can be witnessed on the streets of Apia as well as in the villages. Deaths of children from severe corporal punishment are not uncommon, nor is incest and the above mentioned rape of children. Most of the victims have no one to turn to, as even family members usually support the man who committed the offense, castigating the victim.

In November 2008, the Samoa Victim's Association and its speaker Mr. Josefa Masol took me to one of its shelters for sexually abused children. One of the victims, Apaula (not her real name), told her story which, according to Mr. Masol, is typical in Samoa: "I had been continuously raped by my own biological father for more than a year. The first time I was 15 and he was 53 years old. The first time he forced himself on me, I went to my mom, but she didn't believe me. Mother was simply afraid, or she tried to deny what had happened in order to protect the family and my father's reputation. Before the rape I was a virgin: I showed her blood, explaining what had happened; I begged her to intervene. But she got very upset with me and ordered me to go straight to bed. Then it became routine: my father raped me several times, once holding a knife at my throat. He became more and more violent and as he became jealous he also prevented me from going to school. One day I couldn't take it anymore. I went to school and then I escaped to the police and reported what had happened."

Mr. Josefa Masol explained: "The problem in Samoa is that the great majority is at the bottom level of the capitalist system. The small upper level of society beats them, so they themselves use sticks, keep beating those who are even weaker than themselves—their own children and women. 80% to 90% of Samoans are poor. More than half of Samoan families have to deal with some sort of violence. Sometimes it feels that we are the only organization representing the poor. The poor use us to fight for justice on their behalf."

Apaula's father was eventually arrested and sentenced to 4 years in prison. But he goes home on weekends and when he is released, he will be warmly accepted back by his family. Everybody forgave him. Apaula has no place to go: the shelter is her only future, at least for now. Only one brother comes to see her, secretly. She is the black sheep. The Samoa Victim's Association considers her a 'double victim'. They plan to take her out of the country—to New Zealand—in the hopes for a better future. There are many like her, most are suffering in silence.

"The government doesn't want to talk to us," explained Natalia Pereira, a youth worker for an international organization in Oceania. "They sit down with us and meet us, but they won't act on anything. It is a very difficult country to work in. The only information that we can count on comes from NGOs."

Is it arrogance or complete denial of the problems Samoa is facing? "I can't tell you. But remember, this is not a culture in which you are supposed to question things."

Samoa has a culture of silence. Where breaking the rules is not forgiven. Two former Samoan cabinet ministers were sentenced to death, later commuted to life in prison, in 2000 for the murder of a fellow politician who had threatened to expose a major corruption scandal.

In its dispatch on The US territory—American Samoa—Radio New Zealand International reported on

November 01, 2007:

... The head of American Samoa's criminal investigation bureau says up to 90 percent of child sex abuse cases in the territory go unreported." RNZI quoted Commander Va'aomala Sunia as saying "...the sexual abuse of minors is increasing every year; the vast majority of it happens within families."

In Independent Samoa the situation is much more serious as no outside watchdogs are allowed to bark. The rule of the game is this: if you don't like our way, then get out! It seems that the international community in Apia is fully complacent, busy legitimizing the system. In a tremendously complex area populated by Pacific Island nations, foreign donors and development agencies are desperately trying to create at least one star performer. As the editor Mata'afa Keni Lesa mentioned, Samoa has been designated as that star and, by avoiding almost all scrutiny it gets away with almost everything. Any criticism invariably encounters a standard reply: 'It is our culture and the Samoan Way.'

But what is the Samoan Way—Faa Samoa? The nation is one of the most Americanized anywhere in Oceania, with the exception of outright US colonies, and imported religions are bleeding the nation dry.

"Samoa is indeed very Americanized," says Vavao Fetui, Samoan lecturer at the University of Auckland in New Zealand. "In a way, although it was the first independent country in the Pacific, it is still colonized. There is tremendous propaganda coming from abroad—regarding world politics, for instance."

Anti-Chinese reports put together abroad are regularly

printed in local media. Paradoxically it is China, which provides the most visible and important development projects to the country, for example, constructing government buildings and sport stadiums.

In the meantime, criticism of the US allies, including Indonesia which is violently involved in Oceania through its occupation of West Papua, is diminishing in both Samoas. In July 2009, *Pacnews* reported:

> A United States Congressman has denied that the Obama administration, or Secretary of State Hillary Clinton, has forced him to do a backflip on his advocacy of human rights issues in the Indonesian Province of West Papua. The Congressman for American Samoa, Faleomavaega Eni Hunkin, has become Chairman of the Asia and Pacific subcommittee of Congress's Foreign Relations Committee, and has led a push to remove provisions in a new bill which would have obligated the State Department to report on allegations of human right abuses by Indonesia in the province.

"On Sundays, entire villages speak English," says Natalia Pereira. "All their elites speak English, while bragging about Faa Samoa. Most of their 'half-castes' speak English. Samoa has very strong links to the United States and it is deeply Americanized."

There is probably no other 'independent' country in the Pacific where one can spot sedans and utility vehicles slowly driving through the downtown of the capital city with the US flag flying. Some Samoan members of the government have dual American and Samoan citizenship, including MP

Joe Keil who was recently detained in the USA. In early September 2008, the Samoa Associate Minister was arrested and then charged with representing himself as a US citizen and attempting to use a US passport. In the 1960s Mr Keil was granted American citizenship, and he served for many years in the American Air force, including during the Vietnam War. Eventually a Federal Court judge dismissed all criminal charges against Mr Keil, although no explanation was ever given. This bizarre case triggered uproar in Samoa, and also highlighted the issue of double allegiances and the fact that Samoan men are routinely serving in the American army.

No matter how proud of their country they are on the surface, Samoans are leaving. Hopelessness, stagnation and boredom are some of the main reasons why many opt for emigration. There is not a single bookstore in the entire country of Samoa unless one counts a bible shop which calls itself a bookstore, and there is but one cinema. Samoa may be a paradise for a few mainly retired foreigners who call it home, but it is hardly a paradise for the great majority of Samoa's people, despite the fact that they are constantly bombarded by nationalist and often xenophobic slogans. Fa'a Samoa—the Samoan Way—apparently justifies everything.

Going abroad is often the only escape for enterprising locals, but it often comes with an extremely high price tag. Families whose brightest sons and daughters go to foreign lands expect to be supported and showered with cash and gifts. It is a well-known fact that those who refuse to send large sums of money first receive 'warnings' from family and if they continue to ignore them, next comes the curse designed to destroy health and life of the rebellious ones. Samoa is a very superstitious society and curses are taken seriously.

Naturally, there is a severe brain drain. Almost everyone

who is confident and educated leaves. A country whose main economic activities are remittances and foreign aid is simply unable to hold young and enterprising people.

"Young people in Samoa are very pessimistic and demoralized," explained Natalia Pereira. "Their mentality is as in some Latin American countries: 'go north'! It is not as in Tonga here—in Tonga there is rebellion and revolution in the air, but not here. Here, the attitude of many young people is "if I don't get out of here, I can do nothing and I will be nothing. I will rot here!"

Tourism is becoming an important source of income. With its stunning natural beauty, after Fiji and French Polynesia, Samoa is now the third largest magnet for international tourism in the region. However, as the country is still known for its hostility towards foreign investors, as well as for its lack of transparency and complicated customary laws, its growth is not swift.

When the Twin Otter takes off from Faleolo International Airport in Samoa, the traveler is treated to one of the most beautiful views in the world: the transparent turquoise water of the ocean and its corals, and the enormous island of Savaii with its volcanoes. Then, as the plane slowly turns, rusty tin roofs appear under the wing, together with the unmistakable signs of poverty—garbage and decay.

As it climbs higher, the misery and despair eventually disappear from sight. Below the wings one can observe the thick greenery of tropical forest, enormous gorges and waterfalls unreachable by roads—something one expects to see in Venezuela or Guyana, but not on a relatively small island in the middle of Pacific Ocean. The view of the magnificent ocean world could make one believe that this is indeed the terrestrial Eden. But only viewed from above!

At ground level, driving along the main roads one sees neatly trimmed grass and bushes, and flowers. But it is also possible to detect the reality. Just two kilometers from the center of Apia, driving straight toward the mountains, one finds neighborhoods as poor and miserable as those in the most deprived parts of Africa, with malnutrition, no electricity and no drinking water. These communities often have no names. Visitors don't see them, while local elites do their best to forget about them.

American Samoa is a 30-minute flight away. The largest island where the plane lands, Tutuila, is often described as a green dragon rising from the sea. As with Upolu in Samoa, it is one of the most beautiful places in the Pacific. But it has its own basketful of problems.

The first thing one spots after leaving the airport are enormous signs advertising 24/7 McDonalds, fully equipped with a brand new McCafe. Pizza Hut is across the street. That in itself would not be strange by Pacific Island standards: McDonalds is also one of the main 'attractions' in Apia, Samoa, where it is owned by the former Minister of Tourism. But here in American Samoa the clerk at the car rental agency helpfully confides that Pizza Hut and McCafe are the best places to eat in the country!

Unlike Samoa, American Samoa sees hardly any tourists, a strange phenomenon considering its amazing natural beauty. Advisers, local honeymoon couples and US military are the occupiers of Clarion Tradewinds, the only decent hotel in the territory. To make sure that nobody misses the point that this is to some extent the US, a huge stretch limousine is parked in front of the hotel entrance.

The food is hardly edible even in the restaurant adjacent to the hotel. Local eateries around the airport—the location of choice, as Pago Pago is turning into a tiny 'inner city' in the US urban tradition—offer huge greasy cheeseburgers and mountains of fries. The only relatively healthy dish, a chef's salad, is hidden somewhere on the back of the menu and costs much more than bacon and corn beef, favorites in both Samoas, as well as burgers and anything else that is loaded with cholesterol and calories. Cokes are served Texas style, in something resembling sizeable fuel canisters.

If food is expensive in American Samoa, in Samoa it is simply outrageously overpriced. American Samoa is fully dependent on American imports, Samoa on frozen low quality food from New Zealand, mutton flaps and pigs feet being among the favorites. Spam, some with halal marks, rejected by one of the Arab countries, is considered a delicacy in Apia.

In both Samoas, obesity is common and people, even by US standards, are reaching tremendous proportions. In Apia, I was told that many men die in their 40s. If they make it to 50, it's a sign that they will reach old age. FAO experts with whom I discussed the situation were deeply concerned about the lack of education and awareness among Samoans regarding the food they are consuming. The most serious problem is diabetes and there are cases of amputees.

Although the situation has marginally improved, both Samoa and American Samoa hardly bother to grow anything or to fish. Instead, they depend on remittances and aid, although being a territory of the US, American Samoa is not technically receiving 'foreign aid'. A generally lackluster agricultural sector leads to a situation in which people in Apia and Pago Pago have access to an extremely limited selection of the local fruits and vegetables necessary for a healthy diet.

Five years ago, I had the good fortune to be driven around

American Samoa by Tofoitaufa Sandra King Young, who described herself as "the only public figure in American Samoa who seriously believes that the territory should be aiming at independence." Ms Young was Deputy Director for the Department of Interior's Office of Insular Affairs during the Clinton Administration.

She explained the very negative impact the culture of dependency was having on American Samoa, but noted the difficulty of finding solutions to the problems. Apparently, the Kennedy Administration had been shamed by the US press for 'abandoning the territory,' for investing very little in its social system and infrastructure. A huge influx of funds apparently followed but years later the target of criticism had shifted to the excessive influence that accompanied funds from the mainland.

In the 21st century, American Samoa is a very sad place. With few employment opportunities, there are hundreds of illegal workers. Local youth aimlessly hang around the capital city which increasingly resembles US ghettos: with a population outflow to the suburbs, there are abandoned and burned down buildings, general disrepair, graffiti 'decorating' the walls of houses and a lack of services. The only hotel in downtown had to close one of its wings because of a lack of guests.

Behind barbed wire, the United States Reserve Te'o Soldiers Support Center offers a suicide hotline number posted near the entrance, together with other emergency telephone numbers. American Samoans are dying in disproportionate numbers in Iraq and Afghanistan. It is difficult to compile exact figures but, by the time this report was written, at least 15 American Samoans had died in Iraq. Considering the population of the territory, only 66,000, the death toll is tremendous. Dozens of American Samoan soldiers come back mutilated, while the devastating combat experience leaves its marks on hundreds forever.

On March 5th 2006, when the death toll was much lower, *NBC News* reported that American Samoa is a recruiter's dream. They come around, explaining benefits for the young people to sign on, including such attractive perks as 100 percent paid college tuitions. But the *NBC* reporter summarized:

> Hidden by the staggering beauty of this island is a per capita income that is below the US poverty level. Most wages are low, and there are relatively few employment options for young people. The only big employers are tuna canneries and the government. For many residents, the military is the best—and perhaps, the only—way out … But American Samoa has paid a heavy price … It has the highest per capita death rate of any US state or territory.

Among the victims was 22-year-old Tina Time, who was killed in a desert convoy accident. In the Samoan tradition, her crypt lies in front of the parents' house, bedecked with flowers.

Inside the house, her mother, Mary Time, has erected a memorial shrine, featuring many of Tina's glamour photographs, medals, sympathy cards, and condolence letters from President George W. Bush and Secretary of Defense Donald Rumsfeld.

With three other children in the US military, Mary Time supports American involvement in Iraq—despite her daughter's death.

144

"She didn't die in vain. We need to complete what we started, and I'm with the president that this war is for a good cause," Time says. Looking at her daughter's photographs, and wiping her eyes, she adds, "I miss her, she was a good girl."

In fact the death of Tina Time became a symbol of senseless loss of the lives of so many young Pacific Islanders. One of her obituaries circulating on US blogs talks about her being a bright student and a member of the choir. It also explains to American readers what American Samoa is and where it is located.

In American Samoa, yellow ribbons are everywhere, as well as stickers on car bumpers saying 'Support Our Troops in Iraq.' In one of the most picturesque parts of the island, an enormous banner reads: 'May Peace Be With Our Samoan Soldiers in Iraq. God Bless You All.'

US flags fly in front of supermarkets and private homes. On the streets of Pago Pago, even at the beach, children play with plastic toy machine guns.

One of the most shocking images of American Samoa I encountered was that of a man sitting at the back of the boat plying between Aunu'u Island and Tutuila wearing a T-shirt saying 'NAVY—Celebrate Life,' and turning a toy gun in his hands. Profound depression and confusion engraved his face.

As an old lady on remote Aunu'u Island explained: "Many people want to serve in the US Navy or army. They want to make money but they also want to join the army to escape boredom—to experience adventure. Many people here are very poor, working for $3 an hour. We have over 400 inhabitants on the island, but every week someone leaves for the US. To some it doesn't matter what they are going to do on the mainland, whether they wash dishes or go to the military barracks."

Leaving American Samoa for independent Samoa on the only 'international flight' from Pago Pago, there is, surprisingly, no security check—a security machine is used only for flights to Hawaii. The airport building is old and shabby. This is the same airport where a Hawaiian Airlines Boeing 767 broke a wheel when landing on a runway full of debris a few years ago.

Another magnificent flight provided tremendous vistas, but at both ends of the horizon were two countries divided. Both of them, shockingly poor. By comparison, although not fully free from problems, the regional French colonies are wealthier and more culturally vibrant and upbeat. Regardless of the similarities they share the two Samoas are increasingly growing apart.

Alas, there is no movement on either side that would promote unification. In a few years, the two Samoas and their peoples may become similar only in the nature of their social problems, but too different to call themselves a single nation.

The Kingdom of Tonga and the fight against feudalism in the Pacific Islands

IN THE FIRST WEEK OF MAY 2007, THE KINGDOM OF TONGA was getting ready for a lavish wedding. Seventh in line for the royal throne, Fanetupouvava'u Tuita, 29, was to marry Kiu Kaho, an army lieutenant whose father is a noble, Tu'ivakano, and a cousin of the royal family. Tuita is the second daughter of the controversial millionaire Princess Pilolevu Tuita who runs Tongasat, a satellite communications company, out of Hong Kong.

The Princess's older brother, King George Tupou V, ascended to the throne in 2008. Discussion in the press and on the streets centered on the magnificent 18-karat engagement ring decorated with diamonds. But some Tongan citizens were asking whether this is the way to spend money in a country that has, for some time, been on the brink of financial ruin while consequently suffering from countless social ills. Tonga, an archipelago in the southern Pacific that became a member of the British Commonwealth in 1970 without having been colonized, is bankrupt and troubled. In November 2006, frustrated crowds, predominately consisting of unemployed youths, destroyed most of the downtown area of the capital, Nuku'alofa. At least six lives were lost in the flames of ransacked stores. Some of the rioters were former members of California-based Polynesian gangs deported from the United States. (Crime in Tonga is on the increase and deportees are partially to blame.) Others were allegedly fighting for democracy against an oppressive feudal system.

The opposition has not yet come up with a coherent plan to fight the monarchy and feudalism and even some of the greatest Tongan minds, including the brilliant novelist and thinker Epeli Hau'ofa, do not hide their sympathy for the throne.

Mr. Faleata, who runs a small travel-related business on Vava'u Islands, 400 miles from the capital, doesn't believe that change will arrive through peaceful means: "The entire system, but especially the nobility, is taking advantage of our people. When the rich decide to throw a huge party or to arrange a wedding, the Tongan people have to supply them with food and gifts. What do they get in exchange? Nothing. It is a system of submission and exploitation. In November 2006 we had no riots here in Vava'u. But almost all of our people support the pro-democracy movement. If no changes come soon, the entire country could experience violence on a much larger scale than then."

The Tonga nobility often referred to commoners as me'a

148

vale, 'the ignorant,' but that is rapidly changing. The country has the largest number of PhDs per capita anywhere in the world. Tongans head two regional UN offices, those of FAO and UNESCO. The Tongan poet Konai Helu Thaman, a professor at U.S.P., argues that education was always one of the country's main assets: "Tongans were the first in this part of the world to receive Western education. We had the first mission schools and the first secondary school. For quite some time, education has been compulsory. Families put together whatever money is needed to send their children to good schools. Some see education as an investment: returns come when sons and daughters go abroad, attain good positions and send remittances back home."

Education doesn't only lead to good job prospects. It has also helped to form a relatively large group of inquisitive people, as well as something that is still very rare in Oceania— real opposition. However, the combination of a relatively well-educated population and deepening social problems is explosive.

Epeli Hau'ofa, Tongan writer and thinker raised in Papua New Guinea, wrote in *We Are The Ocean*, a passionate non-fiction book:

> ...Tonga's primogenital inheritance means that younger sons and all women have no inheritance rights to their father's land, unless their fathers control more than one land allotment. Today that means that most Tongans have no inherited legal land rights or holdings, which further means that the growing number of landless Tongans constitute the largest rural and urban proletarian class among the indigenous

populations of our region. Except for those who work in the public sector, and most do not, these members of the new proletariat generally owe little or nothing to the aristocracy and royalty and are therefore generally free of most traditional obligations beyond those to their immediate family circles.

Growing numbers of urban and rural poor see the nobility and the elite in Tongan society as unproductive and corrupt elements.

At the tiny airport of Vava'u, an agent of Airlines Tonga openly insults passengers, both locals and foreigners. She bumps confirmed passengers from the overbooked flight and calls the guard to take away anyone who dares to protest. No compensation is offered, no apology given. "She can do anything she wants," one of the locals explained. "She is a daughter-in-law of the People's Representative from Vava'u. Nobody would dare to suggest that she should be fired."

Back in Nuku'alofa, a member of the 'pro-democracy' movement, Mr. Hapu Mafi, told me: "This government doesn't know what to do. The fact that it is now hiring so many foreign advisors shows that it has no idea how to solve the problems. The majority of our people support the pro-democracy movement, but the PM and ministers are defending the status quo."

"The system which we have now was relevant in the past, but every society needs to evolve. In Tonga, we grew up in a system, which hammered into our brains that the nobles will take full care of society. It worked fine in the subsistence economy, but not in one ruled by the market. These days, nobles do nothing: they just sit in their compounds and take advantage of the majority of our people. We don't want to fully dismantle the monarchy, but even our king should be accountable to the people. The same with the budget: Tongan people are taxed and they are told that to pay taxes is their duty, but the government should also be accountable to the people and be transparent about how the money is being spent."

It often appears that the opposition has clear ideas about the problems the country is facing. However, it is offering very few concrete solutions.

Mr. Hapu Mafi continued: "The pro-democracy movement is also very dissatisfied with the religious leaders who seem to be all too willing to extract funds from families, no matter how poor. Our people are suffering. Inflation is high. The standard of living of Tongans is declining. We don't want to ignite riots. We want to live peacefully. But there has to be some solution to the present problems. And patience is running out."

The mood on the streets of the capital is tense. Groups of unemployed youth gather aimlessly at major intersections. Most downtown shops were leveled to the ground during the November 2006 riots, as was the only multi-screen cinema in the country; one of the very few entertainment outlets on the main island.

Tourism has collapsed almost entirely. The Tongan National Center and National Museum stand almost empty and it is rumored that the complex will be privatized or even closed in 2009. The miniscule expatriate community, consisting mainly of foreign advisers, relief workers and tourists on the way to the outer islands, can be seen only in the handful of surviving cafes.

The park surrounding the War Memorial has been taken over by the Tongan military to protect one of the royal palaces, despite the fact that the King abandoned the ancient palace in the center of the city, moving to a lavish new California-style mansion on the outskirts.

With less than 100,000 inhabitants, the Kingdom of Tonga has more than 450 soldiers in the Tongan Defense Force (TDS) but this is just an official figure. The real number is believed to be as high as 700 and growing. Facing no known international disputes, their primary role is apparently to pacify the population. More significantly, Tonga also sent 40 troops to join the 'Coalition Of The Willing,' supporting the US invasion of Iraq in 2004.

There is talk of training several hundred more soldiers for 'peacekeeping missions'. This is a situation that could easily lead to the same uncontrollable spiral of coups and counter-coups carried out by the military in Fiji. The TDS is partially supported by defense cooperation agreements with both Australia and New Zealand, while the United States military provides training. As such, it is immune to any serious criticism in the local media or in the media of the main regional players. Only humor is allowed: the Minister of Education of Tonga was overheard joking that his country is hiring more soldiers than teachers.

The situation in Tonga is indeed bleak. Unemployment is high and so is inflation. The country has virtually ceased to produce, depending instead for its survival on remittances and foreign aid, together amounting to around 50% of GDP. More Tongans now live abroad than in the Kingdom itself, as is the case in many of the Pacific islands. Their remittances are a major source of income in the islands. Poverty is omnipresent in the capital city, the countryside and the outer islands. And the press is tightly controlled with open criticism of the monarchy taboo.

The Economist visited Tonga in March 2007 and offered this cautiously optimistic assessment:

After a century of royal rule, in which the monarchy defended its power with claims that government by the masses would prove 'corrupt,' political leaders are coming around to the view that more democracy is the best way to check mismanagement and improve Tongans' living standards. Until recently, the cabinet was composed entirely of the king's nominees, and only nine popularly elected representatives sat in the 30-member legislative assembly, alongside nine noble representatives and 12 members appointed by the king. The royal government squandered money on misguided aviation and shipping ventures, and the bulk of the $56m it secured from selling passports was frittered away in poor investments by a visiting American rogue rather quaintly appointed by the king as his 'court jester.' That the royal family also benefited from big private-sector investments— including ownership of the mobile-phone industry, cable television, a brewery and the electricity utility— increased public disquiet. The monarchy responded with a pragmatic reform programme that began before the accession of King George Tupou V to the throne in September 2006. Elected members of parliament were allowed to enter the cabinet, and for the first time in a century a 'commoner,' Fred Sevele, became prime minister.

But Fred Sevele, the Prime Minister, is widely believed to be linked to the royal family by common financial interests and recent reforms have brought few gains to the majority of Tongan citizens. Disappointment with local elites is growing, and tension is palpable in the streets.

A small but influential Tongan intellectual group has expressed disappointment with both the ruling class and the so-called pro-democracy movement. One of them is Ms. Kulala Unu, principal of Tonga High School, an elite institution with 1,400 students that has educated both government officials and leaders of the pro-democracy movement.

"I would like to see much more civic education in my country," Ms. Unu explained. "I would like our people to understand what democracy is and what they want to achieve. Unfortunately, what we saw in November 2006 were just riots. And I hate to say it, but they were mostly ignited by racism. 80% of the downtown area was destroyed, but the original targets were Chinese businesses. This country is receiving substantial help from the People's Republic of China. Even this school was built with Chinese funds. Several Chinese lecturers are teaching here. But there is envy towards hardworking Chinese immigrants. Right after the riots there was talk that several local businessmen paid young kids to destroy Chinese shops."

Some of these 'young kids' were allegedly members of overseas Tongan gangs, deportees from the United States, New Zealand and elsewhere. Educated in racial hatred, mainly against Samoans but also against other ethnic groups, former gang members, according to many Tongans, are adding fuel to the already explosive situation in the country.

Whatever the reasons and whoever the culprit, one of the last feudal strongholds on earth is shaking, its walls crumbling. Tongans have begun to understand that elites are hiding the facts about their exploitation behind slogans like 'tradition and culture'. If Tongans win their fight for democracy, albeit a democracy with its roots in local culture, other impoverished Pacific island mini-states in the region, including Samoa, could follow.

Support from abroad for democratizing changes might be expected. However, the regional powers have long worked closely with local elites. Unfortunately, as long as a country like Tonga votes 'correctly' at the UN, sends soldiers to the right military conflict zones, pledges allegiance to market economics and discourages talk of social justice, the Tongan nobility, royalty and elites can count on silent support from abroad.

In July 2008, King George Tupou V was enthroned in a lavish ceremony that set back the impoverished Tongan state at least US$2.5 million. The coronation was attended by hundreds of dignitaries, including Britain's Duke and Duchess of Gloucester, the Crown Prince of Japan and Princess Sirindhorn of Thailand. The coronation went off without a hitch and without public protest, however, there was some dark sarcasm expressed behind the closed doors of private homes.

In the meantime, before the election, members of the Tongan opposition will have to clarify their own goals. There is no doubt that Tongan elites are corrupt and that the nobility has long exploited the great majority of Tongans—but what kind of society does the opposition want to build? In Tonga, there is no talk yet about 'social justice' and 'equality.' The question of a secular state has still to be raised. Yet it often feels that these words are on the tip of the tongues of many Tongans and that it is just a matter of time before they are pronounced and implemented, and maybe fought for.

Sinking — Tuvalu and the Pacific Islands in an Age of Global Warming

Awell-paved road leads to the northern tip of Fongafale Islet. In some places it is so narrow it feels like a causeway. Fr. Camille Desrosiers slowly drives his van pointing at modest landmarks of his adoptive country. He is 78 years old. Originally from Quebec, he arrived in the Pacific in 1956 and never left, helping the impoverished people, drifting from one small island nation to another: first Samoa, later Tokelau, and now Tuvalu.

Once in a while he slows the vehicle, pointing to a well-constructed house.

"I built this one. And that one."

Asked whether he helped the families get funding for construction he responds with pride:

"I physically built these houses. I rolled up my sleeves, brought my tools and built them."

What the Father built, the sea—unwittingly aided by humans—may not be long in reclaiming.

Eventually the road ends. There is a small turn-around, and then stubs of palm trees, which suddenly give way to endless fields of garbage. Plastic bags mix with rusting metal and unidentifiable pieces of heavy equipment.

As we drive back, the Father notices old women squatting on the coral shore.

"Tuvalu is an environmental disaster. These women look for shells to make necklaces, which they later sell either in the capital or in Fiji. Each necklace is sold for between 2 and 7 dollars, but this practice has to be stopped: the women are killing the creatures, destroying the coral."

He then points at the side of the road: "This road was built from materials imported from Fiji. Now we have weeds that we never had before. They built this beautiful road, but the imported weeds are growing fast, destroying our native vegetation. It's symbolic of what is happening in this country!"

A few kilometers further south appear rusting cars with tropical vegetation filling their interior, growing through floors and seats. Near the shore, an old Korean cargo ship rots, surrounded by coral and the translucent waters of the South Pacific. The shore is also dotted with rusty relics from World War II. Further towards the capital, the road passes lagoons known as 'borrow pits.' These were created during WWII when coral was extracted by the US military for the construction of a runway. Now, several men enjoy a siesta in hammocks hanging next to the garbage-filled lakes as countless pigs roam their shores.

Tuvalu appears to be both a natural and human-made

disaster. Like Kiribati and the Marshall Islands, it is one of the small Pacific Island nations that may eventually become uninhabitable because of rising sea levels which cause flooding, vegetation loss and changes in rain patterns. (Tuvalu fully depends on rain water, having no wells or rivers). Arguably it may be the first nation to disappear from world maps due to global warming, and the one that puts up the least resistance. The sea-level rise has been about 20cm per decade in recent times. Consisting of four reef islands and five atolls, the highest point on Tuvalu is just 5 meters above sea level, with an average of 1-2 meters.

But there are other, even more immediate threats. Rubbish literally chokes this tiny nation and hundreds of men and women are leaving outlying atolls and islands and heading into Funafuti, others are leaving the country altogether, abandoning Tuvalu in the midst of what should be its battle for survival.

Although Tuvalu is spread over 1.3 million square kilometers of the central Pacific, its total surface is only 26 square kilometers, making it the 4th smallest nation on earth after the Vatican, Monaco and Nauru. Nearly half its population of 12,000 is squeezed between the garbage dumps and the deep blue sea in its capital Funafuti, and the government is unable or unwilling to address the problem. Traditional means of livelihood are almost forgotten and the country now fully depends on low-quality imported food, mostly canned. Food packaging is one of the main sources of pollution on Funafuti Atoll. Given that the island has only one 12km road, Fongafale Islet is also being overwhelmed with cars. Many vehicles, including SUVs, are parked in front of the large Taiwan-constructed government building. The capital is also dotted with decomposing fax machines, copiers, scanners and other discarded office equipment. Arriving from abroad as part of foreign aid, this equipment is rarely used and never maintained but is always replaced. The country is fully dependent on foreign aid. Most of the population is involved in subsistence fishing, but the monetary economy is dominated by the government which sells fishing licenses and markets its internet domain name '.tv' but, above all, demands and receives substantial foreign aid. Australia, New Zealand, the UK as well as Japan and South Korea have made major contributions to the Tuvalu Trust Fund, which was set up in 1987 to help the country survive.

All major projects, from a deep water wharf to the hospital and roads were financed by foreign aid, mostly from other foreign governments. Australia is Tuvalu's most significant 'development partner'; total Australian aid to Tuvalu in 2006/07 was budgeted at $5.4 million. According to David Fielding of the University of Otago, NZ, ODA for 1970-2003 was 89 percent of Tuvalu's GDP, compared to 39.7 percent of GDP in neighboring Kiribati, a nation also battered by global warming, overpopulation and social problems. Like almost all nations in the region, Tuvalu plays the lucrative Taiwan/China game: recognizing Taiwan, it receives from Taipei a substantial though undisclosed amount of aid in return.

As a rule, major regional players encourage the dependency on foreign aid by Pacific nations, thereby breeding corruption. The more dependent the country is, the easier it is to control its foreign policy, taking advantage of its votes at international bodies, as well as its strategic geographical location. Aid may be high as a percentage of GDP, but given the miniscule size of some Oceania countries it represents almost negligible amounts for the 'donors'.

The Berlin-based Transparency International described one type of corruption in Tuvalu as 'per diem mentality.' In its 2004 report on Tuvalu it pointed out that:

> ... 'per diem' mentality is ... very much present in the attendance of meetings—e.g. regional meetings, in-country workshops—or other trips oversees.

A ban on foreign travel for government officials imposed by the present administration did not last long. Officials in most Pacific Island nations travel abroad for a substantial part of the year. Despite modest incomes, many officials have residences in Australia or New Zealand and their children often study abroad. Personal gain comes ahead of national interest. Behavior patterns of local government officials and their negative impact on their own countries are, of course, fully known to both 'donor governments' and international organizations, including the United Nations.

Foreign aid keeps flowing regardless of the performance of the local government. While millions of dollars pour into this tiny country, there appears to be no attempt to use the money to address the most pressing issues: garbage keeps piling up and there is no apparent effort to implement waste management programs. No serious attempt is made to save the coral and mangroves—both could slow the process that leads to Tuvalu becoming a group of uninhabitable atolls. Meanwhile, people leave the remote atolls and islands, which lack almost all necessities. Many government officials see no means to solve the country's problems, or at least none consistent with their own personal interests.

The world community naturally sympathizes with this tiny country that may disappear from the middle of Pacific, a victim of the unbridled consumption of industrialized nations translated into global warming. It pays little attention, however, to the fact that support to the local government will do little either to save the nation or to help its people.

If we were looking decades ahead, probably the most effective help would take the form of educational programs, explaining to the people how to defend their shores and attempt to encourage them not to migrate from the outer atolls. But to some, there are other issues that are more immediate. For very little cost, the international community could also help to solve the garbage crises and encourage the planting of mangroves and revitalization of the coral.

Kelesoma Sanoa, the Prime Minister's Personal Assistant, frequently handles environmental issues: "I think that waste is as great a challenge for this country as climate change," he explains. "We have to get serious about waste. It is an enormous problem that we have to face. Our people depend on imports. Their mentality is still that if they throw things on the ground, they will eventually decompose. They are not used to dealing with plastic and metals. There are several illegal dumping sites. We have to change our people's mentality."

Just 3 kilometers southwest of the government building, in an area known as Tekavatoetoe, a young man looks over a 'borrow pit' filled with rubbish. His house is built on stilts and his patio overlooks an enormous deposit of plastic and metal garbage. He declines to use his real name is but ready to assess the situation:

"As you probably noticed, our government has a tendency to blame everything on the people. They say that we lack discipline in making illegal garbage dumps. Almost all the so-called illegal rubbish pits were created by the government or by the Town Council. In this community, we protested and complained for years, but our voices were never heard. Some time ago we had to physically stop the government from dumping more rubbish here. We were ready to fight. Until now, no measures have been taken to clean up our land."

More than an hour's boat ride from Fongafale, idyllic Funafala Islet boasts white sand beaches and coral, and tall palm trees, but in recent decades, this island has lost almost its entire population. Former residents moved to Fongafale and foreign countries, particularly New Zealand. Now only five families remain, surviving on subsistence fishing and crafts.

Folavu is 67 years old. Funafala Islet has been his home his entire life, and he has no intention of moving.

"They keep talking about the rising sea-level, but I don't think we have to leave our island for centuries to come," he says. "Ever since I can remember, people here have built their houses on stilts. Water comes and goes. Last week the waves rolled over the entire island and look, we are still here, and so are our houses. They say that seawater salt destroys agriculture, but we don't cultivate anything here. People of Funafala are fishermen and craftsmen. I was born here and I want to die here, if they let me."

In terms of basic services like drinking water, electricity, transportation, medical care and schools, there is very little help that places like Funafala may expect from the government, which, it seems, wants the local population to move to the main island. For many inhabitants of Tuvalu's outer islands and remote atolls, a move to Fongafale is a first step on a path that eventually leads them out of the country.

Kesia, a middle class employee from the capital, visits Funafala almost every year with her daughter Letisha. They come to admire the serene beauty of the island where Letisha learns from an early age about the traditional life of her threatened nation.

"People come here and take pictures, because they realize that our traditional lifestyle may soon disappear," says Kesia, viewing the lush tropical vegetation. The lively colors offer an almost unreal contrast to the sheer white of sand and coral.

Nearby, an old woman caresses her small granddaughter, both slowly rocking in a hammock hung next to the beach.

"It seems our government thinks if it moves us all to the capital, there will be no need to do anything for the outlying islands. They don't force us to leave: they just do nothing for our communities. And the rising sea-level is an excellent excuse. It also takes much less effort to declare the country to be 'beyond salvation' and then demand aid as compensation, than to try to fight for its survival."

"Some of my neighbors in the capital have already migrated to New Zealand, some to Fiji. In the outer islands like this one, people can hardly resist; they have no schools and no medical centers. Young people are forced to move to the capital to attend school. This way, nobody takes care of the elderly who eventually have to follow. There is only one boat on this island and it is private. To hire it costs 40 Australian dollars one way to get to the capital. Nobody can pay this price and there is no public transportation available. This island used to have well over one hundred inhabitants, now it has only 20 left."

Back in the capital, David Manuela, Centre Director of the University of the South Pacific (U.S.P.) expresses his frustration: "Tuvalu can't withstand the impact of the greenhouse effect. During the recent flood, there were areas that lay 40cm below the sea. At the present speed of rising sea levels, the country can survive only 50 more years. The

United States keeps asking the global community what it is doing to combat terrorism. But I would like to ask, what is it doing to prevent Pacific Island nations from disappearing? Waves are rolling over Tuvalu. It is not our fault that global warming is taking place. The issue is how the rich world can help Tuvalu."

After lamenting, Manuela unveils his plan, which is in fact identical to the government's. According to him, the best solution is relocation: move the people to some Australian islands between PNG and the Northern Territories, give them autonomy and extensive foreign aid. Asked why the people should be moved to Australia, which is not the major polluter, instead of the United States, European Union, Russia, or even China, Manuela responds that Australia is Tuvalu's close friend. This ignores the fact that long serving former Australian conservative Prime Minister John Howard consistently refused to even meet his Tuvalu counterpart and discuss the issue. It seems that Australia feels it is already doing too much for its unfortunate neighbor. Since 2001, only New Zealand has begun accepting Tuvaluans, 75 a year—only those, however, who are under 45 and relatively well educated. This is leading to a brain drain. Australia has not acknowledged the prospect of climate refugees.

There are other major concerns, one of them expressed by Sumeo Silu, director of the National Disaster Management Office: "If we were to face the same situation as Aceh or Southern Thailand, if a tsunami were to hit Tuvalu, our casualty rate would be 100 percent. Nobody would survive. There is a lot of talk about the dangers we face, but not much is being done. It saddens me to say it, but despite everything, Tuvalu is not better prepared to face disasters than it was in the past."

Many leading environmental scientists argue that Tuvalu suffers not only from global warming, but also from other forms of human-made environmental destruction that are wiping out its coral and mangroves, and that it suffers in particular from the unwillingness of its leaders to take the actions needed to avert the disappearance of their country.

Just a few minutes walk from U.S.P. the Assembly Hall of Laopou Village is hosting the annual 'Fatele' dance and music performance. Two large traditional cultural troupes compete against each other in a vibrant, breathtaking spectacle. Tuvalu music and dance traditions are some of the most compelling in Polynesia. Observing the pride and zeal of the performers, it appears highly unlikely that if given the choice, these determined people would be ready to abandon their little country to a bleak fate, without a fight. Despite its size, Tuvalu is undeniably a real country. It has its own language, its own traditions and arts, and is inseparable from its geography and environment.

Espen Ronneberg is less than enthusiastic about the prospects of evacuation of the entire nation. He served as Vice-President of the Kyoto Conference in 1997 that adopted the Kyoto Protocol and is now working as Climate Change Advisor at the Secretariat of the Pacific Environmental Programme (SPREP).

"The bottom line is that small island states like Tuvalu, Kiribati, and the Marshall Islands are very vulnerable to climate variability and extreme weather events right now because of their unique geographic and physical attributes, combined with a number of other factors. But it also has to be acknowledged that a lot of human activity on some islands is very detrimental to the resilience of their natural defense systems."

"My organization is working with these countries to formulate assessments and plans for adapting to climate change, so that near term impacts can be addressed, and so that longer-term impacts can be prepared for. Given the predictions of science, however, it is clear that without strong measures to reduce global greenhouse gas emissions, comprehensive adaptation in many of these islands will be very difficult. Potential evacuation of islands though raises grave concerns over sovereignty rights as well as the unthinkable possibility of entire cultures being damaged or destroyed. We have seen the social impacts on populations internally displaced in the Pacific due to nuclear testing, phosphate mining and other causes and it does not augur well for the future."

According to many government officials, Tuvaluans have no choice: the country has to be evacuated. The majority of the citizens of this atoll nation do not share this opinion. Some don't realize the decision has already been made—in the air-conditioned offices of the government building in the capital. As if to prove the point that nothing can be done to save the country from disappearing, the government fails to 'defend Tuvalu': garbage piles up all over the archipelago, coral mixes with rubbish and is bleached, and mangroves die. And all the while the seawaters inexorably rise.

More than a thousand miles from Tuvalu, Majuro, the main island of RMI, may eventually suffer the same fate as Tuvalu. Water is rising and is visible near the capital. During king tides, hundreds of houses are flooded and the waves roll through the entire narrow land of the island. The only road that basically connects all communities based on Majuro is often cut off by the water at several places, including the low-lying area at the end of the airport runway.

On December 2008, the Marshall Islands experienced some of the worst floods in recent history. On January 2, 2009, the *Australian Broadcasting Corporation* (*ABC*) reported:

> The Marshall Islands is continuing its clean-up after massive waves struck the Pacific atoll nation in the two weeks leading up to Christmas. A combination of high tides and storm surges caused a series of large waves to flood parts of the capital Majuro and some of the outer islands ... At least 20 homes in Majuro were destroyed in the floods, while many more were damaged due to flooding and water-borne debris, and on the outer islands more homes were destroyed or damaged. People living immediately along the coast were the worst affected.
>
> "Some people are still completely displaced and staying with family members," Chief Secretary Caste Nemira said. Mr Nemira added that "the total loss of food crops in some areas occurred when salt water from the floods soaked into the soil and may inhibit crop growth for some time."

And that's the main problem—battered island nations will not 'disappear' under the surface of the ocean as a result of the rising sea level. More precisely, they will not disappear for several centuries or millennia. However, they may simply become uninhabitable if no food can be grown once salt water from the floods destroys the soil. If the atolls are unable to produce food and drinking water, if everything has to be imported, there would simply be no point in living on the islands or atolls of bare coral.

Espen Ronneberg explains: "Some of the atoll countries

around the Pacific are no more than a couple of meters above sea level. They are currently experiencing some very serious king tides and storm surges. These are associated with cyclones and storms that may not impact them directly, but the wave patterns they create tend to go over the top of the atolls leaving salt water behind, which is damaging to crops and to houses and other infrastructure. It also contaminates the fresh water supply if they use well water. Those are some of the very serious impacts that are actually being observed. In some islands if the sea-level rises by as much as scientists are suggesting, there wouldn't really be much possibility of saving them."

In March 2009 a large group of international scientists predicted a much gloomier scenario. On 10 March *BBC World Service* reported:

> The global sea level looks set to rise far higher than forecast because of changes in the polar ice-sheets, a team of researchers has suggested. Scientists at a climate change summit in Copenhagen said earlier UN estimates were too low and that sea levels could rise by a metre or more by 2100.
>
> The projections did not include the potential impact of polar melting and ice breaking off, they added. The implications for millions of people would be 'severe,' they warned. Ten per cent of the world's population—about 600 million people—live in low-lying areas … The UN's Intergovernmental Panel on Climate Change (IPCC), in its 2007 Fourth Assessment Report, had said that the maximum rise in sea level would be in the region of 59cm…

Unlike Tuvalu but to a lesser extent than Kiribati, the Marshall Islands are determined not to go without fight. There are several sound projects to save coral and revitalize mangroves and at the extreme edge of Majuro Atoll there are experimental farms that can make the Marshall Islands self-sufficient in basic food. But the country is in a peculiar position (as described in the earlier chapter dedicated to RMI): while receiving help for its environmental efforts from the United States, RMI is still hosting an enormous long range missile base on one of its atolls of Kwajalein. The military base is spreading pollution all over the area—including the most over-populated island of RMI, Ebeye, which is basically used as the garbage dump of the base—and the impact on the environment, including the coral, is devastating. Needless to say, RMI was battered by US nuclear tests after WWII, with tremendous environmental consequences.

The Marshall Islands was not the only country suffering from floods and storms at the end of 2008 and beginning of 2009. Heavy rains and floods, according to many experts the worst in the last hundred years, had hit several nations of Oceania, including Papua New Guinea and FSM (Federated States of Micronesia). The Solomon Islands lost more than 10 people, and thousands were made homeless. In January 2009, Fiji had a state of emergency, as the heaviest rains in memory hit it. There was loss of lives and substantial damage to its infrastructure. As I was landing in Nadi, the entire town appeared to be under water, its main bridge destroyed. Experts blamed global warming and climate change, but also indiscriminate logging in the hills of Western Viti Levu Island, a similar scenario to that which can be observed all over Oceania, particularly in Papua New Guinea and Solomon Islands.

And then the great tragedy hit: The September 29th, 2009 tsunami spawned by a magnitude 8.3 earthquake killed 34 people in American Samoa, 183 in Samoa and nine in Tonga. One of the most complex countries in Oceania—Kiribati—is the third environmental victim in the region.

"We would say that Kiribati is somewhere in between Tuvalu and the Marshall Islands," explained Nick Foon, Climate Change Unit officer from the Environment & Conservation Division of Kiribati. "We are fighting, but we also have some very serious obstacles to our struggle. Kiribati is facing intensive coastal erosion. I used to work for local government and I realized that the local people are more interested in development than in the environment. Here on Tarawa Atoll, many are more interested in building causeways and sea walls than in protecting and conserving the environment. But sea walls are actually causing erosion and their only purpose is to protect and reclaim the land that belongs to individuals and the families."

Driving the entire length of Tarawa Atoll, the most populated atoll in the country, where the government of Kiribati is located, particularly between Bairiki and Bikenibeu, one can see the devastation wrought by the rising sea level: sea water lies in huge ponds in the middle of the atoll, encircling dead palm trees, their bare, rotting trunks rising toward the blue sky. The sea walls mentioned by Mr. Foon are everywhere, built to push the sea away, but in reality causing erosion and deepening the problem. On the causeway, even during normal high tides, waves reach the road. And at the tip of the atoll, around Betio, where one of the most terrible battles between the US and Japanese forces took place during WWII, the coral is almost entirely devastated. Benino, like Ebeye in RMI, is overpopulated and its people indifferent to environmental issues—survival seems to be uppermost in people's minds. Garbage pits and open dumps are visible along the shore, but I had to agree with Mr. Foon: the situation, although critical, was much better than in Tuvalu. There were obvious attempts made to introduce waste management, including a relatively modern facility near Bairiki, and there was also an impressive, at least by Oceania standards, mangrove-planting project between Temaiku and Bonriki International Airport.

But 'to be better than Tuvalu' is not good enough for many Kiribati officials.

"If you drive south from here," said outspoken Teekoa Letaake, Permanent Secretary of Education of Kiribati, "depending on the tide, you will sometimes be able to see the tips of entire islands that have already disappeared."

I found what she described the next day, near the causeway; little coral hills protruding from the sea. And again, several bare palm trunks, like corpses in a horror film, stood silently and accusatively against the background of stunningly beautiful aquamarine water surrounding the atoll. It was a chilling preview of what may happen to entire nations, if the present trend of environmental neglect in the rich as well as developing countries is not halted and reversed.

"Sometimes we think about our nation disappearing," Nakibae Teuatabo, Climate Change Advisor at Environment & Conservation Division of MELAD of Kiribati told me.

"What does it really mean? If it comes to it, how will it really happen? I think the last people will simply leave because our islands become uninhabitable; because it will not be viable to stay, anymore. It may happen, I would say, 80 years from now. We will simply find that our capacity and resources are decreasing and our means of survival will decrease too. If we don't do anything, that's what awaits us in the future."

171

"But much can be done and some things are already being done. As you saw, we plant mangroves and try to educate our people; to tell them what will happen to our islands if we don't respond. We should constantly monitor the environment, but we should also monitor people's actions. Now the EU is trying to help. Japan is helping with the mangrove projects. We also hope that there will be a change in attitude in the United States. The US has been living for too long in its own world; indifferent towards others."

Entire islands and islets are disappearing from world maps. It often happens far away from the centers of power and commerce, hidden from the inquisitive lenses of mass media cameras. I happened to see it in remote areas of the Solomon Islands and once again I witnessed it in Kiribati. But what I saw was probably just the beginning.

Once pristine, Oceania is suffering from environmental degradation brought to it by geographically distant nations. There are dozens of culprits: the US in Micronesia and the French in Polynesia carried out devastating nuclear testing; Malaysian companies destroyed pristine islands through logging in PNG and the Solomon Islands; international companies are plundering entire islands though mining; Taiwanese, Koreans and Japanese are repeatedly accused of over fishing. Unbridled consumption of energy in developed countries has led to the climate change which is now threatening to destroy entire cultures, atolls and nations.

Recently, Tuvalu made a symbolic gesture. *AP* reported on July 20, 2009:

> The tiny island nation of Tuvalu, already under threat from rising seas caused by global warming, vowed Sunday to do its part for climate change by fueling its

economy entirely from renewable sources by 2020.

The South Pacific nation of 12,000 people is part of a movement of countries and cities committed to going climate neutral. Since February 2008, 10 nations including New Zealand, Pakistan, Iceland and Costa Rica have vowed to reduce their emissions of greenhouse gases as part of a goal of reaching zero emissions in the next decade.

Even in Washington D.C., urgency is felt to some degree. Before leaving the White House in January 2009, President George W. Bush, widely accused of creating environmental havoc, designated as national marine monuments three areas in Oceania, a total of 505,760 sq. km: the Northern Marianas, Rose Atoll in American Samoa and several equatorial islands in the central Pacific Ocean. In terms of size it became the largest marine conservation area in the world, surpassing that of the Northern Hawaiian Islands that had been designated as a national monument two years earlier, banning fishing, oil and gas extraction and tourism from its waters.

Is it enough? Definitely not! But every beginning, no matter how modest, should be welcomed and encouraged. Among experts though, it is understood that the conservation area, large as it is, has been selected partially because it has very little commercial significance.

The time is limited and the tasks ahead are enormous. Once entire nations have to be evacuated from their own land, then for them—for entire civilizations—it will be the end of a history that goes back hundreds and often thousands of years. Such an outcome is absolutely unacceptable. To allow it to happen would be a complete failure for humans as a species. It would prove that we have lost both compassion and rationality.

Fiji's Mercenary Military, the West and the Politics of Coup D'état

MILITARY COUPS, MISMANAGEMENT, INTER-racial violence, the emigration of talented and educated Fijians who lost hope in the future of their country—all these factors triggered the downfall of the country which, not long ago, took for granted high standards of living, including quality education and medical care. While militarism, mainly implanted from abroad, and racial intolerance triggered the collapse, world economic crises, the decline of sugar-cane prices on world markets and natural disasters that struck this nation, all took their toll.

In January 2009, severe storms hit the western part of the main island of Fiji, Viti Levu, destroying homes and infrastructure, effectively cutting off main tourist resorts located on Denerau Island near Nadi. At least 6 people died,

174

some swept away by floodwater.

As I was landing in Fiji on January 11th, from the air the familiar area around the bridge over Nadi River at the entrance to the town of Nadi looked like an enormous sunken ship. People were attempting to move to and from the city. Some were standing on the roofs of submerged vehicles, others holding on to anything that would float.

Roads were swept away, houses looted. Several vehicles were abandoned along the highway, some with broken windows, others simply submerged in water in a ditch. Gangs of young men were roaming the streets of Namaka, Martintar and Nadi.

Even before the floods, the country looked battered, but during and afterwards it suddenly appeared utterly desolate.

The military and its government reacted predictably, erecting roadblocks, a favorite army activity, skills learned during its UN and mercenary service in the Middle East and implemented especially after a coup, and declared a state of emergency and imposed a curfew, allegedly in order to prevent looting. The floods announced further social and economic decline.

Even without the floods, Fiji was uncertain in which direction it was heading. The military coup, which took place on 5th December 2006, was hardly one of its history's bloodiest, but it planted seeds of uncertainty in troubled Fijian soil. On that day, Commodore Josaia (Frank) Voreqe Bainimarama overthrew the elected government of Laisenia Qarase in Fiji's fourth coup d'état in just two decades, promising to end corruption, secure true national independence and above all, guarantee racial equality.

Many in Fiji believe that while some of Commodore Bainimarama's goals are essentially sound—for instance, he

175

proposes to amend the constitution to end discrimination against Indo-Fijians—the means he is using are murky and often destructive to the country and its reputation abroad. As mentioned in previous chapters, most of the media in the entire Oceania region is strongly influenced or directly fed by the news, analyses and dogmas imported from foreign English-speaking regional powers. Even though there was hardly any freedom of press to speak of, Commodore Bainimarama cracked down hard in ways that were without precedent in the entire region. In just 9 months, Fiji deported 3 publishers, all Australians, for alleged political reasons. In an incident in January 2009, Rex Gardner, an Australian publisher of *Fiji Times*, was expelled following a High Court ruling in which the paper was fined for printing a letter criticizing the court's legal backing of the 2006 military coup.

For years, there was clearly not much to look forward to for critics of the government and it is obvious that the interim government still enjoys the support of the majority of Fijians. Commodore Bainimarama, who after the coup became 'Interim Prime Minister', is a seasoned ruler and no new face in the turbulent waters of Fijian politics: he had previously taken control of Fiji after leading a counter-coup in May 2000, before handing over power in July 2000 to President Josefa Iloilo.

It seems that provoking the sole super-power, as well as Australia and New Zealand, has become one of the main joys of Commodore Bainimarama. On July 18th, 2008, he announced that there would be no elections the following year as had been promised earlier. His government said electoral reforms needed to be carried out before Fiji could go to the polls.

Pacific nations suspended Fiji from its regional group, the Pacific Islands Forum—an inter-governmental organization that is, paradoxically, based in Suva, the capital of Fiji. It consists of 14 Pacific Island Nations, plus Australia and New Zealand, two countries that, due to their size and wealth, have decisive voices in the organization. In August 2008, the Forum threatened to suspend Fiji if its leaders did not commit to holding a general election by March 2009. Subsequently, at a special leaders meeting of the Pacific Islands Forum, held in Papua New Guinea in January 2009, Forum leaders changed the deadline to 1st May, by which date Fiji had to set a date for elections before the end of the year 2009. The military government, however, stubbornly rejected all deadlines.

On 2 May 2009, Fiji became the first nation ever suspended from participation in the Pacific Islands Forum.

On 1 September 2009, Fiji was suspended from the Common-wealth of Nations.

In July 2009, PM Commodore Bainimarama promised a 'new modern day constitution before elections in 2014'. This was obviously not good enough for Australia, as *UPI* reported on July 16th 2009:

> Australia's foreign affairs minister is confident that the Pacific Islands Forum will maintain the suspension of Fiji at next month's annual meeting in Cairns. Stephen Smith told Australian media that he believes all 16 members of the forum will remain firm in the face of expected pressure from several countries that recently held talks with Fiji's military regime ...

The coup was followed by sanctions from the European Union and partial sanctions from Australia, with devastating effects on Fiji's vulnerable and stagnating economy. Its economy suffered further when foreign tourists who used to fill Fijian state coffers with desperately needed foreign currency, moved elsewhere, mainly to Samoa which has a reputation of being much more stable.

Diplomatic squabbles involving Fiji have become routine. In July 2007, Mr. Bainimarama accused the United States ambassador of spreading misleading information about his coup, comparing the envoy to a New Zealand diplomat he expelled for allegedly meddling in the country's affairs. Verbal accusations and insults between Wellington, Canberra and Suva go back and forth.

In September 2013, Prime Minister Voreqe Bainimarama made the statement on New Zealand's Radio Tarana, saying the PIF is quote "the play thing of the Aussies and the Kiwis".

Bainimarama has promised elections by September 2014, after which the military should theoretically return to barracks.

What makes Commodore and his miniscule army so confident? Republic of Fiji Military Forces (RFMS) are among the smallest armies in the world, with a total manpower of 3,500 on active duty and 6,000 to 15,000 reservists. Three hundred men serve in the navy. Nevertheless, two regular battalions of the Fiji Infantry Regiment are regularly stationed overseas on peacekeeping duties: the 1st Battalion has been posted to Lebanon, Iraq, and East Timor under UN command, while the 2nd Battalion is stationed in Sinai with the Multinational Force and Observers (MFO). The 3rd Battalion is stationed in the Fijian capital, Suva, and the remaining three are spread throughout the islands.

Nevertheless, this small force has carried out four major coups since Fijian independence in 1970. The country was shaken by two coups in 1987, the mutiny at Queen Elisabeth Barracks in Suva as well as the coup of 2000, prior to the latest coup of December 2006. Earlier coups had devastated Fiji by reopening racial divides between native Melanesian Fijians and Indians whose many ancestors were brought to this country by the British colonial power as slave laborers (or more politely speaking as 'indentured laborers') to work the sugar cane plantations. The first were predominantly Hindus from Calcutta. A later wave of voluntary migrants was predominantly Muslims from Gujarat as well as Sikhs from the Punjab who arrived as traders. In the late 80s, Indo-Fijians were a majority, but racial discrimination, which included laws that prevented Indo-Fijians from owning land, and the coups and accompanying violence, looting of Indian businesses and rape of Indian women, triggered an exodus of thousands of the best-trained professionals. Indo-Fijians again became a minority.

Small as it is, the Fijian military (RFMF) is still larger than any other army of a Pacific island nation and it is extremely well connected to international power brokers. More than 3000 Fijians serve in the British Army. It is also independently wealthy as a result of controlling several mercenary schemes supportive of foreign interventions of both the United States and United Kingdom. Some of the mercenaries were once active members of the Fijian army. The government allows soldiers, particularly officers, to transit from military service to join private security firms, which in turn pay it a fee.

In May 2007, *The Age*, an important Melbourne daily, reported that:

> ...the United Nations has called on Fiji to get tough on firms recruiting mercenaries in the South Pacific

country. In a statement [...] a UN working group called on Fiji to create laws to tackle the problem of mercenaries, and to sign on to the 1989 International Convention Against the Recruitment, Use, Financing and Training of Mercenaries.

The working group notes with concern that in a number of instances the activities carried out by Fijians abroad may qualify as mercenary-related activities, the UN group said.

In 2005, Fijian mercenaries were found working on the Papua New Guinea autonomous island province of Bougainville, where they were reportedly training a private army. The UN said people in Fiji also had been recruited by dubious private security firms to undertake work in Iraq.

In 2007 I was able to interview one of the retired top brass of the Fijian military. As he did not support the most recent coup d'état he preferred to remain anonymous: "The Fijian military had been serving in many conflict zones as a UN peacekeeping force," he explains. "But some of its active or retired members were contracted directly by the UK or the US governments. The Fijian military for instance worked on one Iraq project code-named 'Filous' (the Arabic term for currency exchange). The goal of this project was to exchange Saddam's currency for the new money. Fijian soldiers are very familiar with Arabs and their culture. Our soldiers have served for decades in Lebanon, the Sinai Desert and elsewhere."

"The Fijian military actually expanded through UN peacekeeping operations in Lebanon, in 1978. The UN invited Fiji to join the United Nations Interim Force in Lebanon (UNIFIL). Under the British, Fijians have served in many parts of the world, including Malaya. Our soldiers are known for their excellence. They are trained locally, but also in Australia, New Zealand, the US and the UK. The Fijian military and the US military are very close; we used to have excellent relations. Since the 2006 coup the US has frozen all new co-operation, although existing projects can still continue. Another important issue to mention is that US security companies often directly contract retired Fijian soldiers who then serve in Iraq, Afghanistan and elsewhere. For Fiji it is tremendous business."

It is a well-known fact that for decades Fiji has been a major recruiting ground for mercenaries. At home, the issue is taboo or at least free of criticism. With the money continuing to come back to Fiji, there is little public questioning. In post-September 11 world battlefields, the Fijian military is 'marketing' not only its active duty soldiers and reservists, but also more than 20,000 unemployed former troops. Remittances are essential for the survival of many families. A soldier stationed abroad can send home up to $2,000 dollars a month, a huge amount in Fiji, yet a great bargain for the UK or the US where military personnel with similar experience employed in combat zones can easily cost $50,000 or more a month.

Despite Fiji's eagerness, it is lately becoming more difficult to send soldiers to join the British Army in its operations or elsewhere, although not necessarily on political or moral grounds. In February 2009, *The Mail* reported:

> British Army chiefs are scrapping the active recruitment of foreign troops in favour of Britons who want to escape the credit crunch ... A senior Ministry of Defence (MoD) source said fewer Fijians and Tongans would be recruited, adding: "British recruiting

figures have soared since the credit crunch set in last year. Recruiting from the Pacific islands was a way of filling the gap when we had a real shortfall. But now we're under a lot of Government pressure politically to recruit British first and cut back on troops from all other countries."

Definitely the worst blow to the Fijian military is the UN moratorium reported by *Fiji Times*:

> A United Nations directive will prevent Fiji soldiers from being deployed to new international peacekeeping duties.

The newspaper, quoting what it called a reliable source, said the UN directive allows current peacekeeping duties by Fijian soldiers to continue, but prohibits Fijian forces from participating in new peacekeeping missions.

Fiji's current peacekeeping missions include the Multinational Forces and Observers Sinai (MFO) and the United Nations Assistance Mission for Iraq (UNAMI), where more than 500 Fijian soldiers are serving.

On November 1st 2007, the *Fiji Times* carried an interview, conducted by *Pacific News*, with Sakiusa Raivoce, a retired Fijian colonel and director of Security Support, the largest of the country's six mercenary employment agencies. Raivoce observed that:

> Private armies became a viable commercial enterprise the moment America invaded Iraq... The time is right, and our price is right.

His statements were echoed in the same newspaper (*Fiji Times*) by Lieutenant-Colonel Mosese Tikoitoga, 46, a senior officer in the junta led by Voreqe Bainimarama, and a former UN peacekeeper:

"We made a conscious decision to create an army bigger than we need to generate foreign currency. Our economy has no choice but to build armies, and it's a good business... There are few other foreign investments. If we didn't do this, our people would be in the street creating havoc."

He added that more than 1000 Fijians were stationed throughout the Middle East for private armies under the corporate command of Global Strategies, Triple Canopy, Armor Group International, DynCorp International, Control Solutions and Sandline International.

"Fiji is not a particularly rich country," explained one of Fiji's top international consultants who preferred to remain anonymous. "We need money and frankly we don't care what our soldiers are doing abroad. Killing others, being involved in bad causes? It's not our problem. Sorry for being so blunt, but that's how we feel here."

Many Fijians share similar views.

For years, the Fijian military was given carte blanche by the local population. But now the price is being paid as the army brings its combat-zone practices and morals to the streets of Fijian cities and villages.

Even at the top level, the integrity of some personalities in Fiji armed forces is extremely doubtful. An important case was reported by Fairfax Media and by *Samoa Observer* in January 2009:

A man just freed from serving a sentence for punching and kicking another to death has been reappointed to command in the Fijian Navy. Commander Francis Kean, convicted of manslaughter and sentenced to 18 months jail in October 2007, is brother-in-law of military head and self appointed prime minister Commodore Voreqe Bainimarama. The Fiji military denied it was nepotism. Military spokesman Major Neumi Leweni said Commander Kean, 42, was "the right person for the right job"...

Shortly after the latest coup, the Executive Director of the Fiji Women's Rights Movement (FWRM), Virisila Buadromo and her partner were arrested and taken to the military barracks.

"I was threatened and insulted, beaten and humiliated," she recalled. "Eventually, soldiers threw me on the floor and began jumping on my stomach. Since the coup I have been receiving anonymous phone calls, some of them openly threatening members of our organization with rape."

According to Xavier La Canna of *Adelaide Now*, the regime, which previously warned that it would round up reporters seen to be undermining it, has admitted to having a 'blacklist' of people it will prevent from leaving Fiji.

Joseph Veramu, a leading Fijian novelist and head of the Campus of University of the South Pacific (U.S.P.) in Fiji's second largest city, shares his emotions: "Yes, there is definitely fear. People are suddenly scared to speak out, to make a comment and be overheard by a passer-by. The military has managed to plant small, tiny seeds of fear in our society. And then there is reason for real fear as some people are truly suffering, like those who have taken in, dragged to the military barracks."

Despite the many problems faced by Fiji under its Interim Government, concerns over the possibility of the worst human rights abuses have not materialized. The situation is tense, but people are not disappearing and there have been no recent reports of torture. The military cleared the roadblocks from the streets of Suva and withdrew to their barracks. There are presently proportionately fewer soldiers on the streets of Suva than in Manila or Bangkok. Outright opposition and outspoken critics are being intimidated and sometimes humiliated, but there seems to be no consistent physical violence against them.

The leaders of the 2006 coup gave corruption in government as well as pending legislation to pardon those soldiers involved in the mutiny in 2000 as the main reasons for their action. Junta leaders then called for national reconciliation and a multi-cultural society with equal rights for all groups. That was in sharp contrast to previous coups when the Indian ethnic group suffered mightily. As a result, a substantial part of the population, including a large majority of Indo-Fijians, still supports the current Interim Government.

The interim prime minister said he has to do what is "best for the country and the people,"—beginning with changing the country's race-based voting system.

"We cannot let the financially powerful players in the region dictate to us, when we know what is best for our future," he said, referring to the threat of further sanctions from Australia, New Zealand, European Union and other nations.

"Maybe we lose some now, but in the long run, we will be more independent and confident, and our children will have a lasting multi-racial, cultural and tolerant society they

185

can develop in."

"The situation is absurd," declared Tongan novelist, Epeli Hau'ofa in an interview for this book. Mr. Hau'ofa, was a long time professor at U.S.P. in the capital city of Suva. "A military coup is always bad news, but the recent one in Fiji was at least not racially motivated. On the contrary, leaders of the coup, including Commodore Bainimarama, called for equality for the two main ethnic groups living on these isles—native Fijians and Indo-Fijians. This may be the only, possibly the last, chance for national reconciliation in Fiji."

"The United States and Australia—and Australia is nothing other than the right hand of the United States in this part of the world—are putting great pressure on the interim military government. Sanctions are being imposed, sanctions that are harming simple people, not the elites, not the military. In the meantime, the military—the very same military that carried out four coups in the last two decades— is allowed, even encouraged, to serve in the US and UK controlled areas in the Middle East and Afghanistan."

"The Fijian army was created by the UK after the Second World War," continued Mr. Hau'ofa. "It is simply a mercenary force that was designed to be engaged in conflicts triggered by the US and UK, while allowing native Fijians to make money. I say native Fijians, because it almost exclusively consists of native Fijians. Indians were not invited to join after they sent The Crown to hell during World War II. Today, in Iraq and Afghanistan, Fijian soldier-mercenaries are known as the toughest guards around."

But Fijian mercenaries are not only operating on faraway shores; they are gaining notoriety even in their own region of Melanesia. From the end of 2005, three waves of former Fijian soldiers were either employed or tried to make their way to Bougainville, the breakaway province of Papua New Guinea bordering the Solomon Islands. Nine mercenaries were detained in Bougainville itself and others were arrested by the Solomon Island authorities and deported back to Fiji.

An anecdote often repeated in Suva relates that right after the December 25th 2005 coup d'état, the Fijian military took over the streets of the capital and began erecting roadblocks. There was no real use for the roadblocks, but that's what the military had learned during its service in the Middle East and that is what it began implementing at home.

The military leaders of the United States and the UK should spend at least a few moments studying the wisdom of that story. A small chain of islands in the middle of the Pacific had been designated as supplier of the cannon fodder for the Kingdom because its people were very big and obedient, and they had been excellent warriors in the past. Fijians went to war for money and eventually they stopped questioning whether their involvement in the conflicts was right or wrong. War became their lucrative business.

What kind of society can be raised on such ethics? What can one expect from an army that fights for a fee? It was only a matter of time before it would bring its cynicism and twisted morals to the doorsteps of its own home.

A small nation of 900,000 inhabitants, Fiji does not need an army. It faces no external threat. By implanting it here, the UK did a great wrong to the Fijian people. By using it as it did, the US continued in the same tradition. There should be no sanctions against Fiji. Instead, there should be some compensation for the harm inflicted by the great powers, as well as insistence that Fiji dismantle its military and become, once again, a peaceful nation. Only then can 'real democracy' return once again to this beautiful archipelago.

ESCAPE FROM (THE) PARADISE

THE COOK ISLANDS AND THE PACIFIC ISLAND NATIONS: *Will the last person leaving please turn off the lights?* The beaches with golden sand boast palm trees bending almost to the clear blue sea. Beneath the surface of barely detectable waves, the diverse marine life is fascinating. On hotel terraces, coconut juice cools the refined throats of refined jet setters. Traditional huts rub shoulders with some of the most expensive resorts in the world. Here, in one of the most expensive parts of the world, $500 would hardly sustain a couple for more than a day. Together with neighboring French Polynesia, the Cook Islands have become symbols of hedonistic decadence.

Welcome to Rarotonga—the main island of 'Cooks', a country spanning a huge expanse of the Western Pacific, but with a combined landmass of just 236.7 sq kms. 'Raro' may be the main island of the country, but its coastal road is just a bit over 31kms long.

The Cook Islands, a former New Zealand colony, is a subdued English-speaking answer to its Francophone neighbor, French Polynesia with its chic icon Bora-Bora, one of the most lavishly posh places on earth.

With all that beauty and especially with its tranquil white beaches and the clear warm waters of the ocean with its variety of colorful coral reefs, one would expect an enormous influx of foreigners searching for sun and sea, as well as a local demographic explosion to serve them. But the opposite is true: the Cook Islands are losing people at an alarming rate. And despite the arrival of desperate migrant workers from Fiji, the Philippines and elsewhere—almost 300 were given permanent residency status in 2007, the number of people living here is declining at an alarming rate. According to estimates of the CIA *The World Factbook*—Cook Islands: the population fell to 12,271 in 2008. Older statistics still in circulation claim a total population of the Cook Islands of 18,700, of which 10,000 to 12,000 live in Rarotonga.

According to statistics of the Cook Islands Ministry of Education, as a result of migration between 1996 and 2007, student enrolment in elementary schools decreased by 20%.

There are now 60,000 Cook Islanders living in New Zealand alone.

"I can definitely understand why people are leaving," explained painter Ani Exham-Dun, who owns a small gallery Art@Air Raro and is a New Zealand-born Cook Islander. "There is nothing they can do here. The other day a girl was caught painting graffiti on a wall in the capital. As a punishment, she was told to scrub the graffiti off the wall. Instead of thinking about how to make life for local young people at least a bit more exciting, that's what the government did."

Boredom is, of course, only one of the problems the Cook Islands have to struggle against. With luxury tourism becoming the main source of income, prices have skyrocketed. Food, as in the rest of the Pacific islands, is mostly imported from New Zealand or Australia and exorbitantly expensive. A small bag of cassava chips at the gas station now costs almost US$3 while a milkshake sells for $7 or even $10. But local minimal wages have stagnated at NZ$5 an hour, around US$2.5 at the March 2009 exchange rate.

While the country falls ever deeper into a dependency trap, little is being done to encourage local production,.

"It is evident that the Cook Islands depend on imported food," said Vili A. Fuavao, Sub-Regional Representative for the Pacific & FAO, "but very little food is produced there. Cook Islanders are going abroad in search of job opportunities. Meanwhile, some desperate unemployed people from Fiji and elsewhere are trying to migrate to Cooks."

As Elisabeth Wright-Koteka, Director of the Central Policy and Planning Office of the Prime Minister of Cook Islands explained: "The Cook Islands are one of the best performing countries in the Pacific. Our people want the same standards as New Zealand. But we do not have enough resources to satisfy them. Independence was both a blessing and a curse. It's a blessing because we have our own country and freedom of movement, which is guaranteed by the fact that all of us are in possession of New Zealand passports. Without it, we would be just another Tarawa (in Kiribati)— overpopulated and desperate. And it's a curse because now we don't have enough people and we have to import workers from the Philippines and Fiji, and even that is not enough to fill the gap."

The Cook Islands are not the only country that is losing its most enterprising sons and daughters to richer nations in the area and beyond.

"In the past 40 years the Polynesian island of Niue has experienced a population decline greater than that of any other independent state in the world," John Conell observed in *The Journal of Ethic and Migration Studies* in August 2008. Niue is the country with the smallest population on earth and it continues to drop: according to the CIA *The World Factbook*, from a peak of 5,200 in 1966 to the present 1,444 (2008 census). "More than three-quarters of all Niue-born people live overseas, mainly in New Zealand. The balance continues to shift overseas, mainly because of the presence of kin, education and employment opportunities there."

There are more Samoans and Tongans living abroad than at home. In order to support families at home, these two countries are sending young people to New Zealand, Australia and elsewhere. More than half of the GDP of Tonga is provided by remittances and foreign aid, and Samoa is not far behind. According to Statistics New Zealand, in 2006, Samoans were the largest Pacific ethnic group in New Zealand, making up 131,100 or 49 percent of New Zealand's Pacific population (265,974). The population of independent Samoa is now around 180,000. Over 50,000 Tongans live in New Zealand and tens of thousands more in Australia and the United States, 112,000 live in Tonga itself. In Micronesia the situation is not much different.

According to Jiff Johnson of the *Marshall Islands Journal*, there are presently 52,000 people living in RMI (Republic of Marshall Islands), while some 25,000 have already moved to the United States.

Even tiny Easter Island, a Chilean territory, has more

people on the mainland than at home. At the 2002 census, 2,269 Rapa Nui lived on Easter Island, while 2,378 lived in the mainland of Chile, half of them in the metropolitan area of Santiago, the capital.

Needy people from some of the poorest nations in the Pacific, such as PNG (Papua New Guinea) and the Solomon Islands, find it difficult to obtain visas. Only relatively well off and educated citizens can secure trips to Australia, New Zealand or the United States, leading to a brain drain.

Three Micronesian countries, Palau, RMI and FSM (the Federated States of Micronesia) have 'Compact' agreements with the United States: a deal that brings foreign aid to government coffers, while allowing American military bases to be built on the territory of these nations. In return, citizens of Palau, FSM and RMI can travel to the US and settle there. They can also send their children to study. Many educated ones never come back. Some of the families from Kwajalein Atoll, where the Ronald Reagan Ballistic Missile Defense Test Site (RTS) is located, that receive rent payments from the US government never spend it in the Marshall Islands.

The 2006 Asian Development Bank Study on Remittances in the Pacific arrives at the conclusion that:

> ...migration is very significant in Pacific Island states, especially in Polynesia, primarily as a response to uneven economic and social development. In many Pacific island countries, the remittances that flow from internal and international migrants to family members at home are increasing in growing importance, especially in Polynesia where they often represent the single most prominent component of national income. They reach levels rarely found elsewhere in the world.

But in the Cook Islands, claims Elisabeth Wright-Koteka, migration is not necessarily about remittances. "It is different here than in many other island nations. It is not about escape from the culture as in Samoa or Tonga. It is not necessarily about money. We have a culture of migration. We are sailors. Our whole history is about movement. We used to be a colony of New Zealand and we used to send migrant seasonal workers. Migration became part of our culture, of growing up. Young people always like to go away and experience what it is to live in big cities, in the 'big smoke'. Some come back. The biggest cohort of returnees is that of people in their 40s who have managed to save money abroad and want to start a new life back in the Cook Islands."

The Cook Islands Secretary of Education, John Herrmann, would probably agree, but due to migration he is facing urgent problems: "I am struggling to find secondary school teachers," he said at a meeting with UNESCO representatives. "Many of our teachers have left the country and we are increasingly relying on overseas teachers, particularly on those from New Zealand."

But education is not the only sector suffering from labor shortages—almost the entire country now relies on foreign workers and professionals.

A skilled masseuse in one of the luxury resorts on Muri Beach turns out to be a university-educated economist from Suva, the capital of Fiji. While declining to be identified, she assessed the situation this way: "There are more than 600 Fijians working in the Cook Islands. About one half are employed legally, the other half being overstayers. After the last military coup in Fiji, the situation is extremely bad. Families are breaking apart because they have no means to survive on meager salaries. We are forced to leave. But unlike

Cook Islanders, we only have our Fijian passports and now we need visas to go almost everywhere. The Cook Islands are one of the best countries for us to work. Unlike elsewhere in Polynesia, there is almost no racism here. People are very welcoming and compassionate. Wages are low for them, but excellent for us. Many Cook Islanders are leaving for Australia or New Zealand and there is always a demand for foreign workers. We are simply filling the gap."

While the Cook Islands as a whole are experiencing depopulation, there is also an alarming internal migration, which is devastating the outer islands and atolls of the archipelago. The outer islands are hurting more than the main one. Many adults of Aitutaki and Mangaia have left, first to Rarotonga and then to New Zealand. They were simply unable to find jobs on their atolls and islands. Many have left elderly people behind to care for their small children, a situation almost as desperate as on the outer islands and atolls of the much poorer Polynesian country of Tuvalu.

Some time ago the Government of New Zealand severely cut the Cook Islands civil service and reduced or terminated many subsidies that had helped support the economy. Unemployment soared and wages plummeted, forcing many to seek employment in New Zealand, predominantly in the shipping industry. Given the choice, the vast majority of Cook Islanders don't want to leave New Zealand. Some, however, suffer drug and alcohol addiction or receive a criminal record and have been repatriated.

Paul Panchyshyn, a visitor from Winnipeg, Canada, was alarmed by what he witnessed in Mangaia, one of the outer islands. "Mangaia is an island that has seen its population drop by half in the last decade. There are only about 600 souls left on this unspoiled Pacific gem. It was once an exporter of coffee and pineapples, reportedly the best in all the South Pacific. Cheap exports from Asia and Central America eventually took the market for these cash crops and now what few people live on the island exist solely for the meager tourist dollars."

"While we were on Mangaia, there were rolling blackouts, actually blackouts of 20 hours a day, because diesel was in short supply. We found out later that the one tanker used in the Cook Islands was booked to bring survivor supplies to Aitutaki and thus Mangaians had to go without fuel and fresh supplies for weeks on end, further diminishing their tourist appeal. Mangaians are wonderful people and fiercely loyal to their island and the land of their forefathers. Tere, our guide on a cave tour, said the islanders had been approached numerous times by big resort pitchmen and every time Mangaians turned them away. Considering the population was dwindling so drastically, I asked him why they could turn down such major investment. He said it would be an insult to their ancestors: that Mangaians were connected to their land and they would never sell even an inch of their island to foreign investors. Stubborn, yes. Stupid, no. There are probably few places in the world that have the rugged untouched beauty of Mangaia and it's so refreshing to hear them insist on keeping it that way."

It is obvious that the problem is becoming increasingly severe. Almost all Pacific islands are losing people. Environmental refugees are pouring out of Tuvalu, which may be the first country to become uninhabitable due to rising sea level from global warming. Kiribati is facing similar problems, plus overpopulation and social malaise. And the same can be said of the Republic of the Marshall Islands (RMI) with some of the worst ecological and demographic problems anywhere in the world (mainly as a result of the US nuclear experiments and present day missile range on Kwajalein Atoll).

Social destitution and racial intolerance in the larger Melanesian countries, PNG, Solomon Islands and Fiji, is sending tens of thousands of people to distant shores in search of a better living or simply for survival.

"I left the Cook Islands and went to New Zealand," Elisabeth Wright-Koteka told me, "but I decided to return. I simply like to be here. I like my job, my house. I would like my kids to grow up here, to be Cook Islanders ... What is it, really? Maybe a sense of belonging, something we carry inside. It is abstract. We are like a parrotfish from the long reef—a fish that travels the world but always finds its way home. However, coming back doesn't mean that we stay in one place forever. Maybe our lot is exactly that: a movement between the wide world and the reef."

As she spoke, a light breeze began to penetrate the tropical heat. It was suddenly easier to breath. But the water of the Pacific is slowly rising while more and more people are boarding planes with one-way tickets that will take them far away from the palms, the clear warm water and the quiet nights of unspeakable Polynesian beauty.

Oceania Tourism — LUXURY, MISERY, BATTLEFIELDS AND BONES

"**W**ELCOME TO PARADISE!" WHISPERS THE GORGEOUS Air Tahiti stewardess to the microphone upon touchdown on Bora-Bora. "Welcome to Paradise!" says the Air Pacific flight hostess as the plane touches down at Nadi International Airport in Fiji.

It is 'paradise' almost everywhere in Oceania. From the moment you arrive, the word 'paradise' will be repeated ad nauseam. It will scream from the advertising billboards, from the pages of glossy airline and tourist magazines and brochures.

"Your own slice of paradise at bargain prices."

"Invest in your luxury villa in Paradise."

"Dine in Paradise."

"Dive in Paradise."

"Retire in Paradise."

"Swim with sharks in Paradise."

"Honeymoon in Paradise."

Just a few miles from the center of the second largest Fijian city, Lautoka, child scavengers are working in the middle of an enormous garbage dump, trying to make a living by separating filthy objects with at least some commercial value. They are surrounded by appalling smells, flies and desperate-looking dogs. At the entrance to the dump, a big billboard warns that trespassers will be prosecuted. This spectacle is apparently not for those who come to spend thousands of dollars seeking Eden.

And 'Eden' it is, some 20 miles from Lautoka, on reclaimed land that is called Denarau Island, once a tranquil backwater with mangroves. Or at least it is Eden for those who are willing to travel thousands of miles searching for a sterile world of four and five star chain hotels. Now you can choose from several luxury resorts: Westin, Sofitel, Sheraton, Hilton, Radisson. There is a golf course; there are tennis courts, private luxury villas, marinas, posh steak houses and cafes, souvenir shops and a delicatessen. Every night, visitors are offered lavish shows consisting of semi-traditional 'meke' dances.

It goes without saying that the paradise of the 21st century is not 'public'. After all, it is placed in the post 9-11 world and in post-coup Fiji. It is guarded. It is gated. It has its own armed security personnel. One has to be a foreigner or an extremely rich Fijian or a member of the military whose top brass are both rich and corrupt, earning large sums from 'peace missions' abroad (raking off dollars from sending active-duty or retired soldiers as mercenaries on dubious missions to hotspots all over the world) to have access to this exclusive club—several square miles of manicured lawns and gardens, of perfumed servants and relative safety and security.

One day, just a few miles outside the gate, on the access road to 'Paradise', a young woman was dragged by her hair to the bush and brutally raped. Poverty and frustration fuel a culture of violence. The racial divide between native Fijians and Indo-Fijians is growing. Prices are rising astronomically, making Fiji one of the most expensive countries in the region and therefore on earth.

In January 2009, severe floods devastated the city of Nadi and its surrounding area, cutting off all luxury hotels on Denarau Island for a day or two. While the rich and foreigners were suffering in the lushness of five star hotels, entire communities in the not so fortunate parts of Viti Levu were swept away. Looting broke out and the army declared a state of emergency and a curfew. The absurdity of two extremes, those of great luxury and great misery, in proximity were once again brutally obvious.

Bright yellow catamarans still cruise, although half empty, between Denarau and the splendid Yasawa and Mamanuca Island Groups, sprinklers irrigate golf courses and hotel gardens, and evening shows go on, dancers performing for mesmerized audiences.

As the crime rate skyrockets and security is the main concern in the capital Suva and elsewhere, Fiji is witnessing a new type of mass tourism which can be described as 'gated tourism', or, as in some places, even 'tourism behind barbed wire'. In Asia and Oceania, the trend is already well established in places like Indonesia's Bali and luxury resort areas in India, Sri Lanka, Samoa and Papua New Guinea.

Joseph Veramu, head of the Lautoka Campus of the University of the South Pacific (U.S.P.) and Fiji's leading novelist, was my guide to the local slums as well as to the rich estates. He told me: "The entire situation is obscene. We have new developments here, called 'Fantasy Island'. There is so much poverty in Fiji, but the rich insist on living in their dream world, in their fake gothic and neo-Roman fantasy. Of course the people of Fiji are aware of terrible and deep injustice, but so far they are not able to organize themselves. But that's the story of this part of the world in general."

'Veidogo' means 'swamp', but it is also the name of a new settlement outside Lautoka. Nobody knows exactly how many people live here, as no official census has been conducted in the poorest areas. There is no road connecting Veidogo with the rest of the world. During the rainy season, a narrow path leading to Sireli, a suburb of Lautoka, can easily change into a muddy creek. Houses are built from cartons and plywood; some have metal sheets as roofs. There is no glass in the windows.

"Most of our children don't go to school. And in the rainy season they cannot pass through the dirt. The nearest school is 3 kilometers away," said Ms. Nahalo, a Veidogo slum dweller. "Most people here work at the garbage dump, earning between 50 and 60 Fijian dollars a week (30 to 40 US dollars at the early 2008 exchange rate). This has to sustain an entire family, with prices constantly rising. This settlement doesn't even have electricity and our drinking water is rationed. We receive no help from the military government. Previous governments at least came here and showed some interest, but not this one."

The second largest Fijian island, Vanua Levu, is one hour by plane from Nadi. Although the island is poor, it hosts some of the most exclusive and expensive resorts in the world. One of them, connected with the town of Savusavu by dirt road, is the Jean-Michel Cousteau Fiji Islands Resort. After completing my work on Vanua Levu, I decided to visit the resort and talk to the staff. Surprisingly, the place looked no more exclusive than the luxury chain hotels on Denarau

Island, just smaller. But room rates here start at US$575 dollars, climbing to an astronomical US$2,400 dollars per 'luxury' room per night.

"We are doing well; our occupancy is around 80%, although elsewhere in Fiji tourism is very hard-hit," Greg Taylor, the General Manager, told me. "The military coup last year had almost no impact on bookings; just a few cancellations, but nothing substantial. There are almost no Europeans and no Asians staying here. On average we have 45% Americans and 50% Australian visitors. Those coming from the US never heard about the coup. Those from Australia heard too much about it, are tired of reading about it, and are ready to come to Fiji again."

The taxi driver taking me to and from Jean-Michel Cousteau Fiji Island Resort is not as relaxed about the situation as the general manager. He curses the military, tourists and the situation his people have to endure.

"It is good for the super rich. They come to my miserable town and see how dirty and poor it is. They take some snap-shots of the children on the street, of the market and dilapidated buses. Then they drive on this unpaved road, check into the luxury of the resort, close the door behind them and enjoy feeling so rich and privileged. I think they come here in order to feel the contrast. If they are rich, poor Fiji makes them feel even richer. If they are not rich in Australia or the US, they feel rich in Fiji. Why else would they build so many luxury and exclusive resorts on this struggling island? I heard that they have much more beautiful beaches in Australia and New Zealand and that prices there are lower. So why here?"

It is very difficult for two worlds with such different standards of living to co-exist next to each other in comfort and harmony. Tourists staying at one of the posh resorts can easily spend in 24 hours more than an entire underprivileged Fijian family earns in an entire year. This, naturally, creates tensions. And it is happening not only in Fiji, but all over Southeast Asia, and the South Pacific. Recent political and consequently economic developments have brought gloom and desperation to the islands of Fiji. One has but to look at the faces of ordinary men and women of these beautiful but struggling isles to detect the frustration and fear. But local people are forced to, or paid to, pretend otherwise. They pretend that they are happy, that the greeting 'Bula!' is genuine, that they are the contented and primitive men and women in Paradise. Paradise is what sells. People of paradise are expected to fit the stereotype of being simple, 'friendly', poor but content, always smiling, always ready to please.

There are smiles and seductive looking women on all the brochures promoting French Polynesia—probably the most hedonist travel destination in the world.

"I've lived here for more than a year, but I still take 10 to 20 photos a day," confided Anne Roure, Director of Operations of the five-star boutique Sofitel Motu located on a private island.

A special boat shuttles guests between the island and another Sofitel facility on the Bora Bora mainland. Standing on the hill overlooking the breathtaking Coral Garden, its reefs visible below the turquoise water of the bay, Sofitel is visible, most of its 31 private villas built over the water. Parts of the bedroom floors are made from thick glass, exposing the marine life below. To provide the atmosphere of bliss and chic, the hotel ordered all curtains from Kenzo, while all food served on the premises is presented on fine china and is organic.

"Normally these islands receive 200,000 visitors a year in the territory with fewer than 300,000 inhabitants," Anne Roure added. "Visitors mainly come from the US, but about 40,000 arrive from Japan with substantial numbers from the EU."

"When my contract is over, I will find a way to stay here for ever. There may be the crises in the rest of the world, and business is a bit down even here, but this is still as close as it gets to paradise."

The number of people ready to splurge on exotic and luxury holidays is lower now, due to the world's financial meltdown and economic collapse, but tourism is still the most important part of the economy of French Polynesia. Private jets are parked in front of the small terminal at Bora Bora airport and hundreds of luxury yachts cruise through the crystal clear waters.

However, luxury tourism has not brought prosperity to all sectors of society. Exorbitant prices put many products and services out of reach for substantial numbers of people. The number of French Polynesians living below the poverty line is unknown. There is almost no data available and the territory is one of the worst documented parts of Oceania when it comes to hard statistics. When asked for poverty or extreme poverty in French Polynesia, most official Internet sites simply show N/A.

But there is poverty in the French Oceanic paradise, and it is widespread. There are appalling shantytowns right next to the runway of Faa'a International Airport on Tahiti. It is dangerous to walk after sunset almost anywhere on the main island and as well as general confusion and restlessness there are unmistakable signs of gang culture almost everywhere.

Right across the small stream separating Sofitel Bora Bora Beach Resort from the tiny shantytown, children pull down their shorts and expose themselves to shocked visitors. Some of them make suggestive signs.

Bora Bora is supposed to be the icon of exclusive tourism.

Some of the most expensive and exclusive hotels in the world occupy their own private islands or parts of the outer islands rim, the latest addition being Four Seasons Bora Bora; chalets of several hotels are built right over the water on wooden supports.

Yet driving around the island one sees barefoot, even naked children running in front of their dilapidated dwellings. One wrong turn and a visitor can encounter an open-air garbage dump or shanties that belie the tropical dream.

All over the Pacific there are contrasts as extreme or much worse than those in French Polynesia, which is one of the richest parts of Oceania, with an estimated GDP per capita of $17,500 (PPP for 2003, latest available statistics, CIA *Factbook*). Lavishly priced establishments adjacent to open misery are a sad but normal sight in many countries in Oceania.

The secluded Coconut Beach Club on Samoa's southern coast of Upolu Island is built right next to the dirt-poor Maninoa village. The resort charges around US$300 per night for its over-the-water fales, but has untrained and generally rude staff from the local villages, thus creating a tense and unpleasant environment. (The employment of staff from nearby villages was part of the deal that allowed the resort to operate.) In Maninoa, entire families share basic sanitation, surviving on meager incomes and remittances from relatives working abroad. Little wonder that some locals feel hostile toward the Coconut Beach Club which, while borrowing some elements of traditional Samoan architecture, pampers its guests with a spa and swimming pool, and cleanliness and hygienic standards unreachable for the residents of surrounding villages.

But it is not only stereotypical images of international travel agencies—those of empty white beaches with palm trees—that attract travelers to this part of the world. Oceania is renowned for some of the most unusual tourist destinations in the world. Bloody battlefields, underwater cemeteries, destroyed civilizations and remnants of nuclear experiments dot this vast but sparsely inhabited region.

There is the cemetery of the Japanese fleet near the islands of Chuuk (also known as Truk) in the Federated States of Micronesia (FSM). One internet site promoting tourism in FSM (www.janeresture.com) describes the underwater scene in the following words:

> What lies beneath the blue waters is a submerged museum of World War 2 wrecks, for there are more than 60 ships of the Japanese wartime fleet encrusted with corals lying at various depths. On them are fighter planes still in transport, trucks still lashed to the decks of freighters and officers' china and utensils with brand names still recognizable.

What the site describes is the result of a grizzly chapter of the war in the Pacific. During WW II, Truk Lagoon was Japan's main base in the South Pacific theatre. A significant portion of the Japanese fleet was based there, with its administrative center on Tonoas, south of Weno. In 1944 the US launched Operation Hailstone in which twelve Japanese warships, thirty-two merchant ships and 249 aircraft were destroyed, although larger warships, having received advance warning, were already at sea.

This morbid diving attraction is a magnet for a small but constant flow of divers and snorkelers who every year descend on this most populous island group of FSM (the estimated population is 53,000) to investigate the enormous underwater cemetery.

The Chuuk island group is bankrupt, its infrastructure is in disrepair, and the majority of its population lives in poverty. The only connection with the outside world and with its own capital on the island of Pohnpei is via the US carrier Continental Micronesia. Chuuk's only export is a tiny amount of copra and dried coconut meat. Tourism, no matter how small, is the main source of income.

Tarawa Atoll in Kiribati may be facing some of the most acute problems in Oceania. Overcrowded, worn out by diseases and ecological calamities, it nevertheless offers unlikely visitors several 'spectacular' of WWII battle sites—one of the first and bloodiest in the Pacific—dotted with rusting Japanese cannons, bunkers as well as US military equipment. The most impressive is the Betia War Memorial Park.

It seems that misery is no deterrent for international tourism. There are still diving spots in Marovo Lagoon in the Solomon Islands, which have been devastated by international—mainly Malaysian—logging companies.

Now numerous diving companies advertise trips to Bikini Atoll, which is still largely uninhabitable due to high radiation in locally produced food. Bikini Atoll experienced devastating US nuclear tests in the 1940s and 50s and its population had to be relocated. Bikini Atoll is renowned as a place where the United States performed nuclear experiments on human beings, while destroying an ancient culture. But it is also a place with some of the most stunning wrecks in the world, including the only divable aircraft carrier, the USS Saratoga, and the enormous former flagship of the Japanese Imperial Navy, the Nagato.

Bikini Atoll also offers much more than the usual wrecks for those seeking gruesome spectacles. Diving companies advertise, in an upbeat tone:

At Bikini, you will witness firsthand the effects of a nuclear explosion on warships, as these are the only ships in the world ever sunk by an atomic bomb. These include the USS Arkansas which "From 'D-Day' at Normandy in the Atlantic to the Battles of Iwo Jima and Okinawa in the Pacific, was one of the 'unsinkables' until the Baker test finally brought her to her grave." (quote from http://www.rreinc.com/, the website of Robert Reimers Enterprises, Inc.)

It seems that the past and present suffering in the Pacific is no deterrent. Quite the contrary, it is a magnet, at least for a very small but determined group of travelers and tourists.

The greatest attraction for Australian tourists in Papua New Guinea (PNG), one that triggers 'pilgrimages' of thousands of visitors every year, is the so called Kokoda Trail (also known as Kokoda Track). This is a 96 kilometre long foot trail, renowned as a site of the World War II battle between Japanese and Australian forces. No matter how deteriorated the security situation at Port Moresby, nothing can deter Australian groups seeking to re-live moments of past military glory. Nothing deters the intrepid. Not the security situation, nor the exorbitant $300 that the Crown Plaza, the only passable hotel in town, often charges for its rooms.

When it comes to past bloodletting, nothing can compete, at least not in Micronesia, with the small island of Peleliu in one of the tiniest countries on earth, Palau. Here US and Japanese forces clashed in one of the most brutal battles of WWII. Anticipating carnage, the Japanese military evacuated all local residents to other islands, barricaded themselves in the caves that honeycombed limestone ridges and awaited the US forces, ready to die in the final battle in 1944. The caves became mass coffins as US troops used flamethrowers and grenades to seal them shut. Of the 10,000 Japanese forces only 400 survived, the majority of them Korean laborers. 8,000 Americans lost their lives. The battle lasted two and a half months.

Now Peleliu sees a steady flow of visitors from both Japan and the United States, mainly family members of those who lost their lives on this tiny and remote island.

Travelers are still chasing the remains of the titillating history of Oceania that goes back long centuries. Rapa Nui (Isla de Pascua in Spanish or Easter Island in English) experienced brutal internal battles over natural resources as well as near extermination by Peruvian and European slavers. To the present: fallen idols dot the coast, speaking about bygone eras of unmatched violence.

Back in Fiji, the huge billboard at the Sofitel Hotel in Denarau states that:

... Passengers of shipwrecked canoes were almost always inevitably killed and eaten.

Cannibalism, which was wiped out in Fiji by Christians only 130 years ago, sells. Souvenir stores offer wooden forks that were said to have been used to torture victims and to consume human flesh while the victim was still alive.

The grizzly but titillating account goes on:

Generally, those eaten were enemies killed in war, but other categories of people (conquered people, slaves) could also be legitimately killed to acquire a 'bokola' at any time. This was necessary because certain regular events required human sacrifice: the construction of temples, chief's houses and sacred canoes, or installation rites of a chief ...

"Then, as now, the best cuts went to the chiefs and priests," a bored hotel guest, who had apparently studied cannibalism and modern Fijian politics, commented laconically. "Christians never wiped cannibalism out, anyway. They just changed the menu. The rich here don't have to stick forks into the human body, anymore. There are different ways to kill, destroy or consume human beings."

I don't know the answers to the questions raised by the taxi driver in Savusavu. All I am certain of is that more and more fences, barbed wire and gates are going up in both Asia and the Pacific Island nations.

Every year, tens of thousands of foreign travelers visit old battlefields of Oceania, as well as the ancient sites of great civilizations wiped out centuries ago. While interest in 'history-related tourism' may be growing, there seem to be almost no conclusions drawn by these adventurous travelers. Oceania is arguably the least documented part of the world. Its history serves to entertain, not to send a warning to other parts of our planet. Is international travel helping this part of the world, or is it one of the main causes of the problems this part of the world is facing? Time will tell.

In the meantime, the gap between the rich and the desperately poor is deepening. Indifferent to this fact, new luxury and exclusive hotels, resorts and beach clubs are mushrooming everywhere, from Fiji to Samoa to Vanuatu. Beaches, remnants of ferocious battles, nuclear sites, even past cannibalism are packaged and promoted by mainly foreign companies tirelessly seeking profits.

It seems that everything can be marketed, even misery.

Paradise Lost—Logging and the Environmental and Social Destruction of the Solomon Islands

Alarge fiberglass boat propelled by a 40HP engine speeds across the pristine waters of Marovo Lagoon, a double-barrier enclosed lagoon with hundreds of stunning islets. The area is on UNESCO's provisional world heritage list. Having left Ramata, a small settlement almost at the Northwest extreme of the lagoon, it is heading for New Georgia Island, locally known as the 'mainland' because of its size.

A few minutes after departure, dark stains appear on the surface of the crystal-clear water.

"That's from the logging," explains the skipper, guiding the boat towards Gerasi Camp now clearly visible from the lagoon.

Red-brown gashes of exposed earth cut through luxuriant

green tropical forest. Around noon, the heavy equipment is idle. Although some logging continues in the area, the forests around Gerasi are almost completely destroyed.

LOGGING AND THE ENVIRONMENT

"Gerasi Vao Camp has had between 600 and 700 logs piled up sitting near the jetty for 3 years," commented Curren Rence, a former government official, who now runs the local inn and is one of the elders of Ramata village. "Why did they cut down these trees, if they think they are not good for export? Local people got almost no money from these logs. And we have no idea what the government plans to do with them. They are rotting."

The polluted water of Gerasi Camp penetrates the nearby mangrove area, creating brown streams on an otherwise spotless water surface. Old logging equipment and the Malaysian speedboat Putri Anggrek sit rotting near the shore. Locals try to sell small coconuts to occasional passer-bys. When the clouds move away and a brutally hot sun begins to shine, oil spills become more visible, creating a stunning contrast to the see-through water of Marovo Lagoon.

"Logging still takes place upstream on the Niva River," the skipper told me. "The loggers use chemicals which pollute both the river and the lagoon. It has devastating effects on animals. Crocodiles, which formerly co-existed peacefully with the local people, went mad from poisonous chemicals and the changing environment. They became unpredictable, moving between the islands, attacking people. One woman in our village recently lost her arm. The crocodiles in this area have already killed at least 4 people. Children from the other side of the lagoon commute to Ramata to attend secondary school. They paddle across in small canoes. We see it as a disaster in waiting."

"Foreign, mainly Malaysian companies are coming to the government and to North New Georgia Timber Corporation (NNGTC)," continued Rence. "They use NNGTC as an intermediary between them and the landowners, to get access to customary land. The government doesn't come here—it does nothing to control the process. People in the villages have no idea what's going on. We have already asked one advisor from the Regional Assistance Mission to the Solomon Islands (RAMSI—mainly controlled by Australia) to pass the message to the government. We need the government to take action. The nearest logging site has been in operation for the past 3 years, and the company has already sent away 4 shipments of timber. Last year they paid a meager 400,000 Solomon dollars (about US$50,000)—an amount that has to be divided between two local tribes. What happened to the rest of money?"

International organizations and local inhabitants agree that the involvement of foreign companies—mainly Malaysian belonging principally to the Kumpulan Emas Group, to Rimbunan Hijau, to Golden Springs International, and, to a lesser extent, Korean—has had negative, often devastating, effects on tribal communities all over the Solomons. Environmental destruction arrives together with the culture of corruption. Entire traditional structures in rural tribal areas are collapsing.

Tim George, Special Coordinator of RAMSI, insists: "RAMSI remains very concerned about what is happening with logging in the Solomon Islands. Our concerns are threefold. One is the implication for the country of the current unsustainable rate of logging and the impact of the rapid decline in earnings from logging that is inevitable in the next three to five years as the commercially available trees are logged-out."

"The second is in the area of law and order. One of RAMSI's primary goals was and remains to assist the Solomon Islands authorities to restore law and order as the logging industry is frequently cited as a sector, which fails to comply with the principles of good governance. This is not just a question of simple legality; there are also the potentially costly environmental and social impacts that flow from operations taking place in remote areas that are very difficult to regulate or scrutinize."

"The third and most difficult concern is the impact that logging interests appear to have on political processes here. There have been some encouraging signs from the Sikua government. After several attempts by previous governments, the Sikua Government announced on 25 April that the price for logs that is used to calculate the revenue due to the government in duty on the export of logs, will increase on May 1 and that an authentic formula to keep it in line with world prices is to be put in place."

However, Greenpeace Australia Pacific offers a bleak overview of the current problem. In its April 2008 report 'Securing the Future—An Alternative Plan For Solomon Island Forests And Economy,' it states:

The Solomon Islands has 2.8 million hectares of forests, covering around 85% of the total land area. However, only one fifth (600,000 ha) of the natural forest area is suitable for commercial logging, and all remaining large forest areas (over 50,000 ha) are in poorly accessible hill and mountain areas. The forest has been heavily exploited over the last two decades and current logging is out of control. Industrial logging in the Solomon Islands is dominated by foreign companies who, along with local front companies and contractors, landowner agents and middlemen, and a compliant government, have been logging at a rate that is four times the estimated 'sustainable yield', or the level of non-declining harvest.

Many other reports and assessments have documented financial irregularities such as transfer pricing, misreporting and tax avoidance, serious environmental and social impact, and the fact that logging is economically less beneficial to local landowners than small-scale economic activity. The logging sector currently accounts for 67% of export receipts, 15% of domestic government revenue, and 15% of GDP. However the IMF recently predicted a rapid collapse of logging with commercial natural forests being logged out by 2014. The IMF, the Central Bank and the Governor General of the Solomon Islands have all warned of serious financial, economic and social impacts when this happens. According to some forecasts, economic growth will decline to 1.5% per annum, down from 10% in 2007, largely due to a rapid decline in logging as commercial forests are logged out.

From the speedboat, heading southeast, more and more logging sites are visible. Like scars, they cut through the greenery of tropical forest. One of the largest and most polluted belongs to the Malaysian company Golden Spring. There, white foam hugs the shore and the water is a turgid brown. From the pier, it can be seen that devastation extends towards the hills.

But it is not only large commercial logging that is scarring the islands around Marovo Lagoon. On hundreds of sites, native forests have given way to coconut plantations. "Tribal chiefs and religious leaders in this area decided that coconut trees had to be planted, and everyone had no choice but to follow," explained the skipper, adding that there never seemed to be a real market for coconuts.

Around the Golden Spring logging site, villages and local settlements are controlled by the religious group Christian Fellowship Church (CFC) which believes in full control of its congregations. The church leadership is allegedly benefiting from the logging in the area, promoting highly controversial reforestation projects and introducing oil palm plantations.

Inhabitants of the community near Tita spoke on condition of anonymity: "Most CFC people can't be blamed. They are not free; they have to obey their leaders. It is a tough religious order."

Oil palm plantations are mostly not visible from the shore. I am tipped off about their emergence upstream on the river that passes through Tita. It takes some time to negotiate our entry, before the boat is allowed to proceed toward the local headquarters of CFC. A large villa and a church are at the very edge of a substantial logging site, with oil palm plantations clearly visible. The solid construction of the church and chief's house are in striking contrast to the miserable shacks of the less fortunate inhabitants of the settlement. Half naked children are running around the shore.

It is understood that the money for the churches and villas comes from the Malaysian companies that organize the logging, promising to distribute produce from oil palm plantations later. Help does not always materialize. After the native forest is logged out, the companies often move on, without offering any further assistance to the communities. In Honiara, the nation's capital, Aseri Yalangono, one of the CFC leaders and an employee of the Ministry of Education, told me: "Our community is eager to run reforestation projects. It is true that we plant palm oil, but not only palm oil ... also eucalyptus and mahogany and teak".

Grant Kelly, the Australian owner of the legendary Uepi Island Resort located in one of the most picturesque parts of Marovo Lagoon, commented: "Oil palm plantations take a lot of chemicals. Pesticides and herbicides have to be used. In the past, some people got very sick and had to be flown to the hospital in Honiara."

THE SOCIAL IMPACT OF INTERNATIONAL LOGGING

It seems that voices against industrial logging in Marovo Lagoon speak in unison and it is only the government's unwillingness to act—mainly because of the paybacks it receives from foreign logging companies—that prolongs the agony of Marovo Lagoon and other parts of the Solomon Islands.

People like Grant Kelly are naturally concerned about the environmental impact and the influence it will have on their tourism projects. He also points to many terrible by-products of the logging.

"Logging camps helped to create an atmosphere of lawlessness. There is fighting there, also prostitution of both boys and girls. Not to speak of alcoholism."

Aseri Yalangono agrees: "There are no real benefits for the communities from the logging. Benefits come to only

1% of the population—those who are rich already. Logging companies come with huge bags of money; they often give community leaders 100,000 Solomon dollars (US$12,000). I never saw so much money in my life. But it probably represents only 1% of the amount that they will get from the logging operation. The situation is corrupting our girls: they go to the camps or they are shuttled to the fishing and timber boats from Honiara. There is prostitution, unwanted pregnancies. Malaysians sometimes take underage girls as second wives, abandoning them when it is time to return home. Many terrible things are happening."

Curren Rence, talking me in Ramata village, could not agree more: "They pay us too little. And the money only divides our communities. Our environment is now poisoned, our women, girls and boys sexually exploited, and forests are gone. My question is: why is it allowed to happen?"

According to Greenpeace:

> many serious social impacts resulting from logging have been documented over the last decade. These include: destruction of water sources and desecration of sacred and burial sites, child sexual abuse and prostitution, increased disputes and conflict within a community, the breakdown of social structures, and hardship resulting from the loss and damage to forest resources that local people rely on for their every day living.

Marovo Lagoon is one of the most fascinating areas in the world. Most of its waters are still transparent and its coral is of great beauty, often growing in fantastic profusion only a few feet below the surface. From the air, both water and the islands appear as one haunting entity. But it is much more than just a beautiful collection of snapshots. Marovo Lagoon is the largest salt-water lagoon in the world. It is inhabited by people who speak their own language and have their own history, culture and legends.

The person whom many hold responsible for many of the present problems—Minister for Forestry, Sir Allan Kemakeza—was Prime Minister of the Solomon Islands at a time when many dubious concessions were given to the logging companies.

Asked about the problems related to logging, he replied: "A big problem in the Solomon Islands is that resources are controlled by the land owners. What people want to do with their land and their trees, the government has no control over. It's not like other countries where the government owns the land. In the Solomon Islands, 85% to 90% of the land is customary, owned by the tribe or individuals."

After being pressed further, Sir Allan acknowledged that: "… the present policy of the government is to drastically reduce logging activities in the country. We are almost coming to the end."

Logging, mining and fishing by foreign fleets brought several glaring problems to the Solomons, the most chilling being child prostitution and child pornography. *Time* magazine ran a story 'Sold and abused' on March 27, 2006, claiming that:

> … many visitors are sexually abusing the country's children—and parents, politicians and police seem powerless to stop them.

Sir Allan was ready to remind me that, "in the Solomon Islands there is no age of consent…" although Tania Herbert's report (mentioned in this chapter) claims that the legal age is 15. With a lack of legal protection, there also seems to be an acute lack of will on the part of the government and police to tackle the problem. The problem is well known and documented. So are the departure points of the boats that are taking underage girls to foreign boats docked in the harbor and the logging camps where abuse takes place."

In 2006, when the *Time* report went to press the Solomon Islands didn't have a single patrol boat that could operate at night to intercept vessels that were taking children—girls and boys—to the fishing ships. Now it has two—high-tech and powerful ones. But they sit in the port, idle.

Not much was done even after publishing a comprehensive report 'Commercial Sexual Exploitation of Children In The Solomon Islands: A Report Focusing on the Presence of the Logging Industry in a Remote Region', a report prepared by Tania Herbert of the Christian Care Centre, Church of Melanesia, Solomon Islands, in July 2007. The report found:

> ...child prostitution was the most prominent type of exploitation, with 25 stories collected, affecting 36 children. Children ranged from age 11 through to 19, with most children being aged 13 to 15 years. Most of the perpetrators were foreign loggers. There were 12 stories of children entering into early marriage or being 'sold' into marriage by parents. All but two cases were marriages to foreign loggers, and six stories were about girls below the legal age of 15. In addition, there were two cases where a child was at risk of being trafficked, or sold to be taken to another country. There was also a range of sexual abuse cases, with crimes being committed by both foreign and Solomon Islander men.

Pregnancy of children was an issue, with nine stories of underage girls becoming pregnant …There is little doubt that the presence of the logging company is a contributor to these abuse and exploitation cases with children.

ETHNIC VIOLENCE

The Solomon Islands are in profound crisis. Since 1998 ethnic violence, government misconduct and crime have undermined stability. On July 24th, 2003, an Australian-led multinational force, the Regional Assistance Mission to the Solomon Islands (RAMSI), began arriving in order to restore peace and disarm ethnic militias. RAMSI became an international security contingent of 2,200 police and troops, led by Australia (under the Australian Federal Police and Australian Defense Force named Operation Anode) and New Zealand, and with representatives from six other Pacific nations. Nobody in the region was too happy about Australia getting directly involved militarily, but at that time there seemed to be almost no other solution. Interviewing several government officials at the time of the crisis I came to the conclusion that the Australian initiative was welcomed by many simply because Honiara had no comprehensive plan to solve its own internal conflict.

Although the official count of lives lost during the violence stands at hundreds, some influential figures, including high-level Catholic clergy, claim that as many as 2,000 to 3,000 thousand people died in the conflict.

On 16th April 2006, ethnic Chinese became the main

target of protest riots triggered by rumors that Taiwan had paid for the election of the unpopular Snyder Rini as prime minister. Not distinguishing between Taiwanese and Chinese, the crowd attacked Asian looking people. The Chinatown in the country's capital of Honiara was nearly leveled following looting and arson attacks and some 90% of Chinese-owned businesses in the capital were destroyed. Fearing for their safety, most Chinese evacuated the country. The Solomon Islands have no diplomatic relations with the PRC as it recognizes Taiwan. However, many victims in Chinatown were immigrants from mainland China, some having lived in the Solomon Islands for generations. RAMSI forces did close to nothing to protect the Chinese minority, although the racist riots served as an argument to boost the Australian presence in the Solomon Islands. From 20th April 2006, RAMSI forces were bolstered by a further 220 Australian troops, while New Zealand sent a further rifle company and 30 police officers.

Reconciliation is still a distant dream. Mistrust is dividing regions. Corruption is omnipresent. The economy is dependent on logging, mining and the selling of fishing licenses. And money flowing out of the country is not helping to increase the standards of living of ordinary citizens of the Solomon Islands. As in neighboring PNG, slums are now growing around the once dormant capital, Honiara. Several international organizations have warned that over-logging, over-fishing and mining may lead to environmental and economic disaster. Government officials are doing little to change the situation. Logging continues; so does almost uncontrolled fishing of tuna in the territorial waters. There is gold and diamonds under the rolling hills of the Solomon Islands, and there is nickel. The mining industry is ready to move in to become the next to exploit this country, one of the least developed nations in the world.

For Leliana D. Firisua, Technical Director of the Solomon Islands' Small And Medium Enterprises Council, corruption is one of the main problems that his country faces.

"Our organization is absolutely against logging as it is now. We are only interested in eco-timber and downstream processing of logs, in adding value to the timber. We are all suffering from the corruption here, especially from corruption involving our politicians. But we have to be careful, if you know what I mean. We have freedom of expression, but we have to watch out when criticizing our ministers."

Grant Rosoman, Forest Campaigner from Greenpeace explained why: "There were some casualties. In 1995, for instance, there was the murder of Martin Apa, a local community leader who opposed the logging of Pavuvu Island by the Malaysian company Maving Bros Ltd."

Before leaving Marovo Lagoon, Curren Rence took me for a last spin around Ramata Island. Despite the pollution, there is still more beauty than ugliness. I recall the words of UNESCO science expert Hans Thulstrup: "Even with the forests logged out, Marovo Lagoon deserves to be declared a world heritage site. It satisfies several requirements. Its several distinct ecosystems can be found above and under the surface of the sea."

But just a few minutes from Ramata, I am shown the small Hapu-Hapu islet.

"It sank half way after last year's tsunami," Curren explains. "Right here, there was a beautiful white sand beach. Now it is buried under the sea and you can only see mangroves. There are several islets like this in Marovo Lagoon. It is a direct result of global warming. And what is happening around

here—indiscriminate logging—is adding to the problem."
Ramata airport is just a small wooden shack at the edge of
an unpaved runway. The local residents built it, with almost
no government help. There seems to be very little involvement
from Honiara when it comes to just about anything, from
infrastructure to the fight against brutal logging companies.
Locals say: "We can't expect anything from Honiara. And
we don't. But this time we really need help. Alone, we will not
be able to stop the loggers and the destruction that comes
with them."

PNG—SISTER IN MISERY

In his book *The South Pacific*, Ron Crocombe wrote: "As forests
were depleted in Southeast Asia in the 1970s, loggers turned
to Melanesia. Villagers wanted money, and logging companies
made ridiculous promises, leading innocent villagers to
believe that if they sold their trees, they could all afford cars,
fine houses, modern social services and a life of luxury. The
usual reality has been short-term handouts of alcohol, food
and other petty gifts, trips and treats for leaders, followed by
poverty and deprivation in a devastated environment with
much reduced economic and other potential. The PNG
Commission of Inquiry into the Timber Industry described
some logging companies as 'running the countryside with
the self-assurance of rubber barons, bribing politicians and
leaders, creating disharmony and ignoring laws.'

International—mainly Malaysian logging companies—
are not only extremely active in the Solomon Islands; they are
intensively involved in the exploitation of the neighboring

and sizeable Papua New Guinea (PNG)—the largest and most populous of all Pacific Island nations with an area of 462,840 km² and an estimated population of 6.5 million. Loggers learned to navigate the complex cultural mosaic of PNG—some 850 diverse languages and traditional cultures, and its land ownership regulations and rules, some of which go back several centuries. The loggers most commonly used tool is the corruption of government officials, as well as of tribal chiefs and elders.

Logging and mining have such devastating effects on the environment, demography and welfare of local people that it can't be fully ignored by international organizations or even by mainstream Western media, which, however, tend to focus their attention on Asian markets, conveniently overlooking the fact that Australia and other 'Western' countries are the main destinations of PNG timber.

On February 28, 2006, CNN reported from Sydney (Australia) that:

> The vast majority of logging operations in Papua New Guinea are illegal, environmentally unsustainable and provide little benefit to the country ... The report, by the Washington-based Forest Trends non-profit organization, says logging in Papua New Guinea is dominated by Malaysian-owned companies, whose primary export markets are China, Japan, and South Korea. Once processed, many of the logs are exported to Europe and North America. Forest Trends says corruption is having a devastating affect on PNG living standards and calls on big importers of PNG timber such as China to take a 'global leadership' role in overcoming illegal logging. The report is based on a

five-year external review commissioned by the World Bank and the PNG government. It said that a study of 14 logging projects covering 3.17 million hectares found all were operating illegally and the harvested timber was not being sustainably managed.

On June 11th, 2009 *Pacnews* reported from Canberra:

> Environmentalists are asking Australia to honour a promised ban on an estimated AUD$400 million (US$320 million) worth of illegal timber imports each year, reports Radio Australia. The environmental lobby group, Greenpeace, and an Australian Greens Senator, have accused the government of Prime Minister Kevin Rudd of backing away from its election pledge.
>
> And they have support from a former Papua New Guinea conservation department official, Lester Seri, who now represents Conservation Melanesia. He said poor governance and corruption continue to drive illegal logging in his country, and said Australia was complicit if it doesn't ban imports from the trade …

In 2001, one of PNG's leading newspapers, *The Nation*, using its customarily colorful language, predicted the end of illegal logging in an article 'World Bank study will put nail in coffin for PNG logging industry.' The article began with an optimistic summary:

> The World Bank seems hell-bent on destroying Papua New Guinea's commercial logging industry with its latest device involving a review of the forest revenue system by six experts.

Seven years later, logging continues full speed and it is widely believed that *The Nation* is now owned by one of the Malaysian logging companies.

In June 2008, The Australian reported that:

> Papua New Guinea is losing its accessible forests so quickly to logging and farming that more than 80 per cent will be gone within 13 years. A five-year study by experts from the Australian National University and the University of Papua New Guinea Remote Sensing Centre has found PNG is losing 362,400 ha of forest a year, equivalent to 1.4 per cent of its land area.

That was just a few months after I locked myself in a dusty office in Port Moresby with Demien Ase, chief lawyer of the Center for Environmental Law and Community Rights, Inc. (CELCOR), an organization that represents many victims of intimidation by logging and mining companies, and also chairman of Eco Forest Forum (EFF), an umbrella for the forestry environmental groups in PNG. I listened for hours to his systematic *j'accuse* against the activities of international logging companies in his country.

"Malaysian companies here are corrupting our officials," Mr. Ase declared. "Those they can't bribe they intimidate, particularly the Rimbunan Hijau Group, which is one of the largest Malaysian multi-industry companies. They use torture, hanging people upside down, beating them, and forcing men to sodomize each other. They use police officers for their designs, the same as in Sarawak in Borneo where they took land from indigenous people. Here they own the daily newspaper *The National* and they own Tropic Air airline as well as several ships. They also own the country's top leaders, funding elections for most of the politicians. They give money to many projects, some dubious. And in exchange they 'only' want logging concessions."

Apparently the EU Parliament, alarmed by the situation, is trying to put pressure on the government. To what extent, it still remains to be seen.

"We work with several organizations in the UK and Holland," continued Mr. Ase. "We also work with Friends of the Earth, Malaysia. But we are not getting any help from the Malaysian government. Although we have written several official letters to the Prime Minister of Malaysia, asking him to force the companies from his country to operate in the framework of law, we have never received a reply. We opened several legal cases against the foreign companies, but they have some of the best lawyers from Australia."

The spite of the Malaysian government toward the victims of logging companies goes back for decades and is well documented. In his *Malaysian Politicians Say the Darndest Things Volume 1*, the famous Malaysian writer and filmmaker Amir Muhammad quotes *The New Internationalist,* which documented in January 1988 Amar James Wong, Sarawak's Minister of Environment and Tourism and a timber tycoon speaking at a meeting he had with an international mission on native rights and rainforest: "The best way to improve your golf is to chop down rainforest… We get too much rain in Sarawak—it stops me playing golf."

In the same book, Amir Muhammad quotes former Malaysian Prime Minister Dr. Mahathir Mohamad and his written reply to a 10-year old English boy, Darrell Abercrombie, who had sent him a letter urging him to stop deforestation because the boy wanted to study tropical animals in the forest when he grew up. (August 15th 1987):

It is disgraceful that you should be used by adults for the purpose of trying to shame us ... The timber industry helps hundreds of thousands of poor people in Malaysia. Are they supposed to remain poor because you want to study tropical animals? If you don't want us to cut down our forests, tell your father to tell the rich countries like Britain to pay more for the timber they buy from us.

With such a mindset towards its own deforestation, it is very hard to imagine that Malaysian politicians and public would show compassion for the victims in Papua New Guinea and Solomon Islands.

There are several parts of the country that are almost completely logged-out, including East Awin near the border with Indonesian-occupied West Papua. This area faces several profound problems, including a continuous influx of refugees from West Papua—there is a refugee camp and the community of refugees numbers around 2,500. According to local officials, East Awin is now almost logged out after concessions were given to the Rimbunan Hijau Group. However, the worst deforestation took place in New Britain and in Vanimo.

Mining in PNG is as devastating as logging. UNEP reported:

...a cyanide spill on 21 March, 2000. A one tonne crate of sodium cyanide pellets was dropped from a helicopter sling during transport operations to the Tolukuma Mine in Papua New Guinea. The incident happened approximately 85 kilometers to the north of Port Moresby over rugged, inaccessible terrain. The

Tolukuma Mine is located approximately 100 kilometers north of Port Moresby and is owned and operated by an Australian company, Dome Resources N.L.

As early as in 1999, the *Asia Times* and other media were reporting environmental rows over the Tedi nickel mine whose tailings were dumped into the sea along the country's northern coast for many years. Cases of environmental damage by mining companies are very common. For international companies it is usually cheaper to bribe officials than to implement international safety and environmental standards.

Many multi-national mining companies count billions of dollars a year in profits from their mining activities in Papua New Guinea. There is Lihir Gold Limited, an international, predominantly Australian, gold mining company with operations on Lihir Island in PNG, Australia and South Africa. The Lihir gold mine holds some of the largest gold resources in the world, around 40 million ounces. There is also New Guinea Gold, a Canadian company, and Rio Tinto, the multi-national company with headquarters in the UK and Australia. The same can be said about what's happening across the border in Papua, where there are several large multi-national companies operating, including the controversial US-owned Freeport-McMoRan.

In both parts of the island of Papua, those opposing the mining projects are regularly killed, tortured, intimidated or simply disappeared. The environmental impact is devastating and so is the culture of corruption surrounding most of the mining and logging projects. Unless journalists are invited to participate in organized visits and are accompanied by representatives of the company, the government or both, the international press has no access to the areas of mining on either side of the border.

To illustrate the urgency of the problem, I quote the address of Jethro Tulin of the Akali Tange Association Inc. in Porgera Enga Province, PNG. This was made as 'A Statement to the UN Permanent Forum on Indigenous Issues,' Eighth Session on May 20th 2009 in New York:

> Madam Chair, this is my second time at this UN forum, and today my message and recommendations are more urgent than before. In my homeland in the highlands of Papua New Guinea, the Ipili and Engan people have seen their traditions turned upside-down by the influence of a large-scale mining project. In one generation, the mine has brought militarization, corruption, and environmental devastation to a land that previously knew only subsistence farming and alluvial mining.
>
> Last year, I explained that mine guards and police were killing locals and raping our women; there have been five more killings and many more rapes since. Last year, I described how our food sources were threatened by mine waste dumped directly into the river system and how my people were exposed to dangerous chemicals like cyanide and mercury; today, those practices continue. Last year, I complained that the mine is directly next to our homes; and just three weeks ago, the Papua New Guinea government, motivated by reports presented by the mining company, unleashed a 'State of Emergency,' a police and military operation that saw hundreds of homes of indigenous land owners surrounding the open pit mine razed to the ground.

The increasing global power and influence of trans-national companies like the Canadian Barrick Gold, managers of the Porgera mine, means that they, alongside the PNG government, must be responsible for upholding human rights within their spheres of influence ...

Poor and geographically isolated, PNG and the Solomon Islands are far from the inquisitive eyes of the world's public. International companies have taken advantage of the weak legal and political systems of these Melanesian nations, unscrupulously plundering their natural resources, undermining democracy and ruining their culture. Foreign military forces or police will do very little to help. The international community should put pressure on the large logging and mining companies active in these two countries, forcing them to operate within the international legal framework.

Unless the people and their land are prioritized over profits, PNG and the Solomon Islands will continue to see their forests disappear, their rivers and coastline destroyed by chemicals and other pollutants, women and children forced into prostitution, even sex slavery. And the world will not only keep losing its 'lungs'—the tropical forests—but also some of the world's most stunning islands, inhabited by unique and, in some areas, still uncorrupt cultures.

Kiribati — To Stand or Sink?

T HE CHILDREN OF TARAWA ATOLL CAME TO PLAY in and around the old bunkers, cabin interiors, and rusty Japanese cannons from World War II. Some sat, chatting on the eerie crooked structures; others risked injury sliding to the very end of long gun barrels, performing acrobatic tricks dozens of feet above the ground. Posing for infrequent visitors, they screamed and laughed. The girls wrestled each other as in American war movies; while the boys made gestures with their hands, gang symbols, or—shockingly—outright sexually explicit ones.

Their playground, now called the Betia War Memorial Park, was the most important site of the first US offensive in the central Pacific, the Battle of Tarawa that began on November 20th 1943 and ended three days later, with enormous casualties on both sides, totaling close to 6,400 US, Japanese and Korean war dead.

Writing after the war, Marine General Holland M. Smith asked: "Was Tarawa worth it? My answer is unqualified: No. From the very beginning the decision of the Joint Chiefs to seize Tarawa was a mistake and from their initial mistake grew the terrible drama of errors, errors of omission rather than commission, resulting in these needless casualties."

Today Tarawa—the most populated atoll in the Republic of Kiribati and one of the most densely populated places in Oceania—exemplifies almost everything that has gone wrong in this part of the world: from unhealthy food to environmental degradation, from reliance on outside help to land disputes, from child prostitution, the spread of HIV/AIDS and leprosy medical emergencies.

The coastline around Tarawa Historic Park is covered by the flotsam of garbage and carcasses of fish, damaged coral, metal bars and scrap, with rotting shipwrecks on the horizon.

Geographically isolated, Tarawa Atoll is Melanesian and Polynesian, but in reality it is living in its own realm, at its own pace, connected with the rest of the world by infrequent flights to Nadi, Fiji—almost 3 hours away by air.

Kiribati with less than 100,000 inhabitants consists of 33 atolls. Its total land area is only 811 sq km, but its span is enormous—3.5 million sq. km. of the Pacific. The distance between Tarawa Atoll and Christmas Island is around 1,500 miles and the boat service is irregular and unsafe, while the air connection is almost never available.

Kiribati is also one of the three countries that may in the near future disappear from the face of the earth due to global warming; the other two are Tuvalu and the Republic of the Marshall Islands (RMI). But long before that, it may experience all sorts of emergencies, and as a result it is sending thousands of disgruntled citizens abroad, who are searching for a better and longer life.

Teekoa Letaake, Permanent Secretary of Education at Kiribati, told me: "You will see, when you go inside the settlements, that Southern Tarawa is probably the worst we've got here. People are living on top of each other. Our government services, especially social services, are barely coping. The schools are overwhelmed. And that's here: but we also have problems on the outer islands."

Soon after we talk, I go to see with my own eyes, but it is not so unfamiliar. Similar overcrowded and desperate conditions can be observed at Ebeye (RMI), just a stone's throw from the US missile base on the island of Kwajalein. Here and there, barefoot children play in and with the garbage while adults sit aimlessly, staring straight ahead as if waiting for something to arrive and rescue them from their poisonous idleness. Beer bottles are everywhere, some simply empty, others smashed to bits.

At Bikenibeu hospital, a team of 15 Cuban doctors is fighting an uphill battle against the enormous scale of ailments and diseases this small place has accumulated.

"Cuban doctors are not simply admired here," said Teraira Bangao, Director of Health of Kiribati. "They are loved. We are truly grateful to Cuba: we only pay small allowances for their doctors, as well as lodging. Doctors come on average for 2 years. Cuba pays for their tickets and salaries. They are so successful and so much accepted by our society that other countries—particularly Vanuatu and Samoa—will be seeking their assistance in the near future."

Mauricio, head of the Cuban medical mission, is not allowed to talk on the record without authorization, but he is not a press attache; he is a doctor. And the work of the team speaks for itself. "Where does it hurt?" is the first question asked by the Cubans in the emergency room. Unlike in so many clinics all over Oceania, money is not discussed nor exchanged. And as in so many countries all over the world where Cuban doctors work, there is an aura of dignity, compassion and extremely high professionalism surrounding their work.

Just across from the emergency room of the hospital—the main workplace of the Cuban doctors—a small Diabetic Clinic reveals how desperate the health situation in Kiribati really is. The clinic has one simple hospital bed and extremely basic equipment for testing. It is staffed by Karote Tauroba, the sister in charge, and by Miiri Tong, a nurse.

"Around 60% of those who are tested have diabetes," explains Ms. Tauroba. "Most of those who are diagnosed with diabetes have at least some basic idea what it is, as so many people around them are already living with it. The number of people with diabetes is increasing. Just here, we register 40 to 60 new cases a month."

The walls of the room are plastered with optimistic foreign posters advertising healthy living for diabetics: vegetables and fruits, mainly. I ponder the sad irony of this country whose diet is almost exclusively dominated by imported junk food.

"We advise patients not to eat too much sugar and salt," says Ms. Miiri Tong. "We tell them to try to avoid white rice. They often look at us in shock: 'Then what are we supposed to eat?' It is true. Maybe they can eat local breadfruit and papaya, but they can't survive just on that, or on local fish. Sometimes we just give up and tell them to at least drink water and avoid all those over sugary carbonated drinks. Sometimes it feels like an uphill battle: in our culture, old people are not expected to do anything. But those with diabetes need to move and exercise. Food that our people eat now has nothing to do with our traditional diet; it is very unhealthy. And our people also have serious alcohol problems."

Sixty percent may seem a lot, but according to official statistics from the Ministry of Health, 779 new cases were recorded between January and November 2008. Yet in some parts of Oceania, particularly the Federated States of Micronesia (FSM), over 90% of the adult population is diabetic, for the very reasons described by Ms. Tong.

But diabetes is not the only condition that is battering Kiribati. At the entrance to Bairiki town, a horrifying poster shows a man exposing the breasts of a woman in what is supposed to be an outburst of lust. Next to them, a morbid skull symbolizes the HIV/AIDS epidemic. Kiribati, it is assumed, has one of the highest HIV/AIDS rates in Oceania, although official statistics speak of just over 50 documented cases.

"We started a very strong campaign," explained Teraira Bangao, Director of Health in Kiribati. "I myself am an HIV doctor. Officially we have 54 cases but some have already died. The reason the number of HIV cases is high is because so many of our men work as sailors, mainly on German boats, traveling the world. We also have serious problems with the crews of Korean fishing vessels operating in our waters—they take some of our girls on board as prostitutes. Then, and I have to be frank; it is also because of our own government officials who travel abroad all the time. This includes people like myself. I travel 5 times a year on average."

"Whatever official statistics say," said Ms. Teekoa Letaake. "The number of HIV cases is much higher than 100. It is suspected that, after Papua New Guinea and the Solomon Islands, we have the 3rd most serious problem in Oceania."

Searching for the well-hidden Climate Change Unit in

Bikenibeu, to my surprise I stumbled on the Leprosy Clinic. I discovered that the fact that Kiribati faces a serious leprosy problem is no secret here, nor does it surprise anyone. The statistics unit at the Ministry of Health could not come up with precise data, but said that the government operates with the following numbers: 34 new cases in 2005 and 41 new cases in 2006.

"Recently we had consultants come from New Zealand," Dr. Bangao told me, "and they said that Kiribati is on the alert for leprosy. Leprosy here disappeared earlier, but then it came back again. People are living on top of each other and disease spreads easily. Moreover, leprosy is extremely contagious."

One of the few consolations is that medical care is free in Kiribati. Even HIV drugs are free of charge, courtesy of Global Fund. Diabetic drugs and even lancets, a 'small knife used to make incisions', surely a strange way … to measure sugar levels are free. The Director of Health explained that sometimes he flies personally to Fiji or elsewhere to bring more precious medicine back.

The sky is blue and the ocean around Tarawa Atoll almost transparent. But it is often said that Kiribati—this enormous country with a tiny landmass—is a microcosm of all the problems faced by Oceania. To reach it, like reaching Nauru—another nearly collapsed country in the Northern Pacific—is arduous and extremely costly, notably because several air links have collapsed.

Sometimes the problems seem overwhelming so that even local movers and doers lose courage and stamina. And the situation is not much different in several other island nations of Oceania: Nauru, Niue, Solomon Islands, even the largest—Papua New Guinea.

"We often talk about the opportunities that could arrive with tourism," laments Ms. Teekoa Letaake. "But who would come to Kiribati? Who would want to stay here? In Fiji perhaps some people would stay, but here? Honestly, even people like you, people who live and work in this part of the world; they come for a few days or a few weeks and then leave. And they rarely come back."

It is true that, apart from Cuban doctors, a miniscule diplomatic and international NGO community and an even tinier group of foreign business people, it is very difficult to stumble over foreigners, let alone tourists.

The Australian travel guide *Lonely Planet* in its South Pacific & Micronesia edition puts it bluntly:

> Being a visitor to Kiribati is hard work but it can be rich and rewarding once you're past the (literally) hot-and-bothered stage. Tourism, where it exists at all, is in its infancy here; in fact, as the locals don't really understand why tourists want to visit or what they want to see or do, even the notion of tourism is a bit weird.

The perception that Kiribati fails at anything its people touch is widespread.

"Of course we would love to have more flights connecting our islands with the rest of the world," continued Ms. Letaake.

"But we already had our own airline—mostly domestic but we had one—and it failed. It collapsed. And foreign investment: our government is doing everything in order to discourage it. We don't invest in infrastructure. We have patrol boats—gifts from Australia and New Zealand—mostly to strengthen 'governance' and to discourage illegal fishing. But when people on our outer islands get sick, it gets pathetic.

Planes don't fly and boats, some quite big, don't sail. Almost nothing works. That's why even the Peace Corps decided to withdraw, worrying about the safety of their staff, especially those based on outer islands."

At Betio, across the island from the place where the children were playing on the cannons and in the bunkers from WWII, a long concrete jetty penetrates the calm surface of the ocean. It is the main port of the country with several medium size ocean vessels tied to the shore. Sunsets here are magical and eerie at the same time, as there are several wrecks rotting near the shore, some looking just ordinary, but others like haunted skeletons left to their lot in the middle the sea.

There are a few local companies with offices near the docks, including Kiribati Copra Mill Company. Copra became the main export of the country after all the rich Banaba phosphate reserves had been exhausted, suspiciously around 1979 when Kiribati finally gained independence from the UK.

As in Honiara in the Solomon Islands, there are always fishing boats near the coast, mainly from Asian countries and particularly from South Korea. Local girls, some barely 18 and others much younger, hang around the ships. As at the Betio War Memorial Park, young girls scream at strangers:

"Hey, Fuck Me! Do me!"

Unfortunately, there is no need for them to repeat it for the foreign fishing crews.

"Child prostitution is a major problem here, as in the Solomon Islands," explained Ms. Letaake. "Smaller fishing vessels come near Bairiki and unload their catch to mother boats—much larger vessels. Most fishermen don't even come ashore. They order girls who are taken to the ships. Girls often disappear for several days, even weeks. Some even live on the boats, permanently. I am talking mainly about South Korean vessels, but there are US ships, too. Within the last 10 years it became big problem here. We have a lot of prostitution, child prostitution, diseases and the child abuse that come with it. Unfortunately, many local parents encourage this, as it is very lucrative. And it is not always fisherman. When 50 Japanese workers were building a causeway in Southern Tarawa, locals say that approximately the same number of children with Japanese features was born during their stay or after their departure. But in that case, everything was done very discreetly and there was compensation and no abuse."

Kiribati is facing some of the most complex problems in Oceania, but it is by no means the only country in peril.

Traveling in almost all the countries and territories of Oceania, I witnessed environmental and social problems of monumental proportions. I do not want to compare these problems to those in Africa, Indonesia or the Philippines— Oceania is geographically too different from the countries on the mainland or those of much larger islands—but there are many similarities. Measured by GDP per capita (but not always on a PPP basis), the Pacific countries are much richer than most other poor parts of the world. But many of their problems are similar. They are as diverse as malnutrition, poor health and education, environmental devastation, child abuse and ethnic intolerance.

In his book *The South Pacific*, Ron Crocombe wrote:

> Micronesia and Polynesia were among the most disease-free areas of the world because the common infectious diseases could not survive in isolation ... Melanesia was less fortunate, being closer to the complex disease patterns of Asia ... Traditional foods

were in most cases nutritious and in ample supply. Producing them involved exercise which kept people fit ... Diets were generally adequate and often excellent, but some places lacked some nutrients, and even fertile islands suffered after hurricanes, droughts or wars ...

However, with the arrival of the colonial powers Oceania experienced a health disaster that was magnified by the social, political, economic and cultural setbacks that accompanied it. Not only did foreigners bring a wide range of diseases, and not only the syphilis that was infamously imported by Gauguin to Polynesia; the entire lifestyle was forcibly changed. Sea voyagers and fishermen were put to work in European-owned mines or in the service of colonial administrations. Oceanian development was severely disrupted and irreversibly changed with wide-ranging social consequences.

Trade, advances in medicine and improved understanding of nutrition make better health possible, continues Ron Crocombe. A wide variety of foods normally improves nutrition, but advertising drives demand for junk food and contributes to new problems ... Pacific people, especially in urban areas, now have some of the world's highest rates of malnutrition, anemia, obesity, cardiovascular disease, hypertension, diabetes, gout, cancer and dental disease. This alarming development is related to a shift from fresh traditional plant and animal foods and breastfeeding to nutritionally inferior highly processed imported foods...

"In the Pacific, around 80% of the people still live in rural areas," Dr. Vili Fuavao, head of the Pacific sub-regional FAO office told me. "They are mainly subsistence farmers. Instead of helping them, we are making great efforts to address the needs of 20% of the population—those who live in urban areas. I believe that we have to strengthen and make more efficient subsistence farmers, instead of pushing people somewhere where they don't belong. In Kiribati and Tonga, for instance, there is a big drive in this direction ... Look at foreign aid: it often focusses on strategy and planning. But we often notice that the most vulnerable families ask for some seeds to get started. We at FAO are now trying to fill the needs of subsistence farmers."

By helping subsistence farmers in Oceania, the FAO and other organizations can help to increase diversity of food all over the region. That doesn't only mean better and more diverse menus for local people. In the local context it means saving thousands of lives.

"When you drive to the airport in Samoa," said Dr. Fuavao, "you see posters warning about the danger of HIV/AIDS. But hundreds more people are killed every year by non-communicable diseases than by HIV/AIDS. Non-communicable diseases are linked to the food we eat. Most of the people that are losing lives on these islands die from nutrition-related diseases. Many of them are treatable. Most of them are preventable."

In the Namosi Highlands in Fiji, I heard of many farmers who are returning to traditional crops and fishing for river clams. As food prices in 2008 skyrocketed, most of them had no choice. While expensive resorts on the coast were still flying in mostly processed food from Australia and New Zealand, local farmers were rediscovering the delights of an organic and simple traditional diet. Fiji was not the only country experiencing such trends. But the question is whether this trend will continue, and whether it will be allowed to continue by those who provide aid while at the same time controlling food distribution and transportation chains.

Education is another serious problem facing Oceania. Although successful on paper and often the single main outlet for government spending in several Pacific countries, education often consists of a medley of confusing and contradictory attempts to bring Oceania into the modern era while preserving a mix of its traditional culture and imported religion. Those who receive education often want to leave the islands, a pattern reinforced by Australia and New Zealand who draw qualified workers from Oceania, often disregarding the region's need for them.

Many larger and poorer countries in Oceania, such as Papua New Guinea (PNG), the Solomon Islands and Vanuatu, are struggling to keep children in the schools. While education is free on paper, parents are often hit with hidden costs and fees. As a result, the illiteracy rate in PNG is around 50%.

"The way forward, in my opinion, is to embrace informal or non-formal education that has already existed in family and village settings," said Yayoi Segi, an Education Advisor working for UNESCO who spent 5 years working in almost all Oceania countries. "Schooling is important but must not be the only pathway for learning. Education is all about what is called the Four Pillars of Learning: learning to know, learning to be, learning to do and learning to live together. It is not about being taught to do so. For countries where access remains a challenge, community based learning must be explored. In fact, this is happening in part of Papua New Guinea. One should acknowledge that countries have human, technical and financial resources that can be tapped into, without having to depend on external sources all the time."

Each administration seems to care more about official balance sheets and saving face than in achieving gains through long-term planning.

"Soul-searching is necessary for Pacific Islands," continued Ms. Segi. "Where do we want to be in 2050? What is our goal? What are our targets? What types of resources do we need? Where to source them? Who do we need to work together with? If there is no paradigm shift occurring sooner rather than lat   er, Pacific Island countries will always struggle, rather than thrive. Ultimately, the failures of education can be blamed for all society's ills."

Visesio Pongi, head of the Pacific regional office of UNESCO and an experienced educator from Tonga said: "The relevance and appropriateness of education is a huge problem in the Pacific. There is very little evidence of strong direction in the education systems of Pacific island countries. They do not seem to have targets and do not know where they want to go; they are merely floating around. If there is no 180-degree turn-around, you will find them in exactly the same position as they are now. So many of the ills and problems Pacific societies face can be directly addressed through education. While countries focus on academic aspects of education driven by exams, the system produces so many dropouts with very little pathway for those who do not find traditional schooling appealing or relevant."

Then there is religion, which, although it arrived with colonialism, makes claims of being part of the local culture, particularly in Polynesian countries like Samoa. Christian religions often employ medieval tactics such as intimidation and calls for total obedience. They also force believers to support the lavish lifestyle of clergy, often openly humiliating churchgoers who donate less then the average. It is not uncommon in countries such as Samoa for believers to steal or borrow money, or simply beg for funds from relatives living abroad in order to fulfill 'duties' towards clergy.

Another severe problem in Polynesia is child abuse and incest, particularly in Samoa, and also in several parts of Melanesia.

"It is a great shame," Epeli Hau'ofa commented, "but in our societies child abuse is extremely high and tolerated. It is not always about sex—it is also about power."

The spokesperson of the Samoa Victim's Association, Josefa Masol said: "Most families here beat their children, that's the local method to socialize them. Around half of the families here experience domestic violence…"

"The Pacific region is sitting on a social, political, and economic time bomb fuelled by unfolding human rights crises," said Amnesty International as it launched its global report, Amnesty International Report 2009: State of the World's Human Rights.

Patrick Holmes, Chief Executive Officer of Amnesty International, Aotearoa (New Zealand) said: "Unlawful killings, media repression, widespread violence against women, and the inability of governments to provide basic services such as access to health and housing in the Pacific in the last year are part of the Pacific's untold story."

Historically known as one of the most peaceful parts of the world, Oceania is becoming alarmingly violent. There have been outbursts of ethnic tension verging on civil war in both the Solomon Islands and Papua New Guinea (PNG). Port Moresby, the capital of PNG, is often described as one of the world's most dangerous cities. Suva, the capital of Fiji, competes with Port Moresby as the most dangerous city in Oceania. And Tonga recently experienced riots that leveled a large part of the downtown of its capital city.

Crime in many parts of Oceania is under-reported and statistics do not always exist. While the US State Department site officially lists Samoa as a safe country, its local newspaper carries an average of one story a week about grizzly murders and rapes. Anecdotal evidence suggests that non-violent crime in Samoa is extremely high. One international worker in Apia reported that her house was broken into more than 20 times during a relatively short stay in the country. Stealing or 'borrowing' has become embedded in the culture.

What is particularly alarming is the dramatic increase in violence. A number of members of Tongan and Samoan gangs were deported from the United States and they are now regrouping in their native countries, a situation not unlike that which long plagued Central America, particularly Honduras and El Salvador.

"It is really incredible what is happening," said Natalia Pereira, a youth worker from Latin America working for an international organization in Oceania. "Young kids, Samoans, killing Tongans in the United States, and vice versa. They say it is 'because Samoans always hated Tongans and Tongans always hated Samoans.' As we speak now here in Apia, they are settling scores somewhere in Salt Lake City, Utah. 'I am gonna kill you because you are a friggin Tongan!' they say. But you know what is really unbelievable? Many of them don't even speak Samoan, or Tongan, only English. Some have never stepped on Samoan soil."

"It is bizarre: I recently interviewed a Tongan boy returning to Tonga who used to kill on the basis of an ethnicity he knew nothing about! Then there are gangs in this part of the world as well, gangs like the Sons of Samoa (SOS) in Auckland, New Zealand. And since 1996, these young people, confused and idle, are being deported from Australia and New Zealand. They are coming back! I recently talked to a boy like that: he was enormous and solid. He could kill you with his bare hands. Push him to the limit and he would crack your neck. He spent most of his time in prison. Some deportees allegedly participated in the riots in Tonga. Of course they made scapegoats of them, but they took part in rioting."

Lack of education and frustration in the communities often lead to the weakest and most vulnerable—women, children or ethnic minorities—becoming victims of extreme violence. To illustrate: in PNG, HIV/AIDS patients are periodically buried alive.

Violence and health problems, poor school attendance and child abuse: all this has its roots in the poverty of the region.

"Most of the people who are experiencing violence at home are from poor families," explained Mr. Josefa Masol. "In Samoa, 80%-90% percent of people are poor. And they are living in the tough capitalist system here…"

But Samoa is one of the richer parts of Oceania. The great majority of those living in Papua New Guinea (PNG) and the Solomon Islands and Vanuatu are extremely poor.

Despite the glitzy hotels on some islands, as previously pointed out by Pacific FAO head Vili Fuavao, the great majority of this part of the world are subsistence farmers.

Foreign-educated local elites take full advantage of the melange of capitalist, feudal and religious systems imposed on their countries to control the local population.

Slums dot the pristine islands of Oceania. The biggest

ones are around Port Moresby in PNG and around Suva, the capital of Fiji. But they are everywhere: on Ebeye Island near the US missile base on Kwajalein Atoll (Marshall Islands); in Tahiti, French Polynesia; and in the backwaters of Samoa and the Federated States of Micronesia. Children running around without shoes and often stark naked is a common occurrence throughout the Pacific. Communal huts where up to 3 generations live and sleep together with no walls or hygiene facilities are still common in many of the countries, often even glorified as part of the 'culture'—not that the rich would ever consider living this kind of life!

Despite the severity of the social and economic crisis confronting Oceania, there is no challenge to the market fundamentalist system within the region. Although there is widespread criticism of the control exercised by the United States, Australia, New Zealand and other Western countries over the independent countries of Oceania, as well as of remaining colonies, there seems to be no organized movement or systematic resistance to the plundering of the islands and their imposed dependence on foreign powers. Dissent, if one can give such a label to the few voices of discontent, is fragmented, isolated and often misunderstood.

News about regional powers bullying Pacific nations into free-market agreements and into competitive environments small countries could not be able to withstand is once again stirring fears all over Oceania.

Epoch Times recently reported:

> Tactics employed by Australia and New Zealand to push Pacific Island countries into signing a free trade agreement are a form of 'contemporary colonization,' said academic and respected analyst on Pacific Island

affairs, Professor Jane Kelsey at a seminar in Auckland last week.

And this from a *Pacnews* report:

> Pacific Island officials involved in the Pacific Agreement on Closer Economic Relations (PACER) negotiations with Australia and New Zealand are worried that they are being pressured into signing an agreement that they do not fully understand, she said…
>
> At a Forum Leader's meeting in Niue, Australian Trade Minister Simon Crean pushed for free trade negotiations (PACER-Plus) to begin at this year's Pacific Leaders Forum in Cairns. Trade officials were given a mandate to devise a plan for negotiations to begin. This, experts say, signaled a more aggressive approach…
>
> "Academics in the Pacific are predicting that 80 percent of Pacific manufacturing could close down under PACER-Plus," said PANG last November, "leading to unemployment for thousands of workers" …
>
> "Most Pacific countries lack secure social nets, such as state welfare, to assist unemployed workers" …
>
> "These expected outcomes of PACER-Plus could leave many Pacific people faced with a bleak future." …
>
> Vanuatu Minister for Internal Affairs, Patrick Crowby said the issue cannot be fast-tracked if advisory institutions are not set up.
>
> "How will the government fund its essential public services if we lose out on vital revenue? Depend on aid donor money? I don't think so," he said to the *Vanuatu*

Post recently ...

"I asked young people in Samoa whether they see their future in Samoa or outside Samoa?" said Natalia Pereira. "9 out of 10 answered: outside. But one stood up and challenged me: What 'future'? Overall, all over the Pacific, there is this mentality: 'The islands will sink anyway, so what the hell!'" Environmental damage throughout the region, much of it inflicted from abroad, is enormous.

And some islands actually are sinking—in Tuvalu, Kiribati, and the Marshall Islands but also in the Solomon Islands and elsewhere—all as a result of climate change in the form of global warming. International logging companies have destroyed most of the forests of the Solomon Islands and Papua New Guinea, while international fleets over fish all over the vast territory of Oceania. Phosphates are gone in Nauru, a country that is presently completely bankrupt, and Kiribati. Many lagoons and coastal waters are polluted and becoming more so daily, wrote Ron Crocombe in *The South Pacific*. Off Ebeye Islet, where Marshallese who work on the US missile range at Kwajalein live, the lagoon was found to carry up to 25,000 times the level of contamination considered safe by WHO ...

Nuclear tests were performed by the US in the Marshall Islands, by the French at Moruroa and Fangataufa Atolls (1966-96) and by the British around Kiritimati (during tests in the late '50s, islanders were not evacuated) and Malden (site of the first British H-bomb tests, Operation Grapple, in 1957). Large areas of Oceania are still uninhabitable because of these tests.

Kwajalein Atoll is still used as a US military facility— eleven of the 97 islands are leased by the United States and are part of the Ronald Reagan Ballistic Missile Defense Test Site (RTS). And although this book is not addressing grievances pertaining to most of the US territories, the recent build-up of the bases in Guam will introduce vast new problems.

Opencast nickel mining scars the French territory of New Caledonia. Gold and copper mining in Fiji, the Solomon Islands and Papua New Guinea (and, of course, across the border in West Papua occupied and plundered by foreign mining companies through the deals Indonesia's dictator Suharto signed) are devastating the environment and bleeding Oceania of its precious natural resources. Profits flow abroad, proving the point that it is actually Oceania that is 'sponsoring' and feeding rich nations and their multi-national companies, not the other way around.

While the Labor government in Australia has done almost nothing to improve its country's treatment of Oceania and its people, the conservative government in New Zealand does not even try to hide the cynicism of its regional policy: New Zealand's Minister of Foreign Affairs, Murray McCully, announced earlier this year that foreign aid would no longer be directed to 'poverty elimination' but linked to trade and economic development and should be compatible with New Zealand's foreign policy.

It often seems that Oceania is doomed—sinking under the tremendous weight of its insoluble problems. Indebted and poor, dependent and not really self-governed yet not true colonies; the islands and people of Oceania are at a crossroads. Many local people recognize that foreign advisers are not there to help or at least not advising too well, that they somehow seek advantages for themselves and for their own countries, not for Oceania. But how can Oceania achieve freedom and reject harmful advice if funds are attached to their presence, if the funds are allocated mainly to the advisers themselves and the local elites? And is freedom still possible? Neocolonial control over the islands of Oceania is complex and elaborate, perfected through centuries of tricks facilitating plunder exercised by Western countries all over the world.

Oceania was once free. It governed itself and fed its people without asking for outside help. Its people sailed thousands of miles from their own shores, discovering new islands, waging battles and wars, forging peace. Life was once firmly in control of those who were born and lived here.

Now, however, the majority of local people have become strangers on their own islands. Oceania is being ruled by laws and principles imported from abroad. Religion, political structure, food, and even many cultural elements are imported now, from far away. From too far away, many would say.

Not long ago, after Oceania's resources had been plundered, its environment severely damaged, and its economies subordinated to international capital, and there was no prospect that local people could regain their autonomy after centuries of colonial rule, the people of Oceania were allowed to rule their islands once again. However, this was only to a degree, with local elites subordinate to foreign governments and capital, and with a particular economic system, within the framework of 'nation states' owing allegiance to the Western powers and their presupposed political interests.

This is where Oceania stands today: at a crossroads. It is too late to go back, but it is widely recognized that continuing on the same path as before will ensure the disappearance of entire cultures, entire islands, and further subordination. Water is rising. And the people are leaving from virtually all countries in the Pacific for much bigger island-nations and especially to other, larger and richer countries. They are leaving for the very places that earlier took away their identity and their means to survive independently. There is still no unity forged among the islands of Oceania, no common goal, and no concrete plan. It will have to come soon. Otherwise the children of those who in the past broke the fragile universe of Oceania will soon irreversibly monopolize ownership over the future of both the islands and the entire Ocean.

When I was in Tarawa, I learned that my favorite writer from Oceania, Epeli Hau'ofa, had passed away in Fiji. We were supposed to meet again a few days later, at the long table of the Barrister Cafe on the campus of U.S.P. in Suva, a table that overlooks stunning tropical vegetation and tranquil pathways. As there was no earlier flight from Kiribati to Nadi, I missed his funeral by only one day. Instead, at the same table I met his close friend and colleague, the great Tongan poet Konai Helu Thaman. But the memories proved to be too vivid and too painful and we decided to move inside the cafe. Epeli was such a giant of Pacific literature and thought that this time much of our conversation centered around him:

"As Epeli would say ...,"

"Epeli believed that ..."

In just one week I would depart from Oceania for good. This part of the world that had become so dear to me was struggling with the same profound problems I encountered when I arrived six years ago; and Epeli had just passed away. There was little to celebrate!

Later, while finishing writing this book, each time I felt overwhelmed by hopelessness, I would recall that Oceania is much more than a long list of seemingly insoluble problems. Injured and off course, tied-up and exploited, it was still forming its own enormous universe, now often barely detectable but profound, endless and stunningly beautiful. It was a universe certainly worth defending and worth fighting for.

Oceania is bleeding, but it is alive. And it is an obligation of those of us who know and love it to speak up, to write about the pain and injustice it is experiencing. Political correctness (a damaging form of self-censorship) has the effect of muzzling analysis and argument, resulting in the simplification of issues and a block on the discussion of controversial topics. According to its unwritten rules, everybody is good and all the problems are manageable. Such an approach serves those who are in charge and profiting from the system, not its victims, the vast majority of the people of Oceania. The opposite approach is urgently needed.

This part of the world needs open discussion, a painful intellectual journey, questioning and challenging its 'new identity'—religion, consumerism, and dependency on former and present colonial masters, which is so much at odds with its traditional values. It needs to define the role that local elites played and continue to play, profiting from the plunder of the region's natural resources and making Oceania subservient to foreign powers. Are indigenous leaders serving their constituents, or are they mainly collaborating with foreign powers hostile to the interests of Oceania? Or does the truth lie somewhere in between? Instead of self-congratulatory speeches, Oceania needs to face its past and present fearlessly and independently. Only by understanding the history of recent centuries, will it be able to address its weighty problems.

To start with, instead of erecting memorials to those who died fighting imported wars on its territory, Oceania should build monuments to those massacred by the US, French, British, Japanese, Germans and others who are still in control in this part of the world. This would be a good first step toward both reconciliation and real self-governance and independence.

After learning about Epeli's death, I drove through the entire southern part of Tarawa Atoll. Beginning at Betio, I crossed the causeway to Bairiki and continued to Nanikai, Ambo, Eita, passing humble dwellings, walls of reclaimed land that were accelerating the 'sinking' of the island, food stores mainly selling junk food, garbage, disappearing islets off the coast, barefoot children. In my mind, as I drove by Bikenibeu and the hospital I saluted the Cuban doctors for doing what they were trained to do—curing people and relieving them from pain. There was the US Coastguard Hercules transport plane on the tarmac of Bonriki Airport and several military men marching toward the tiny terminal, a common occurrence all over Oceania.

I drove further, crossing small bridges over still rivers. Suddenly I came to an abrupt stop, almost at the edge of the bridge leading to another islet. It had collapsed some time ago, its right edge falling toward the water, but locals were still using it, walking close to the left side, risking sliding down but determined to cross. I parked my car and followed them.

On the other side, the scenery changed. Traditional dwellings were surrounded by impenetrable jungle. The road I walked on now had nothing in common with the overcrowded streets of South Tarawa. So near, and yet the feeling was like that of the outer islands.

I had no idea where I was and I didn't care; it didn't matter. An old beat-up truck gave me a lift, bringing me to the small jetty. I boarded a small-motorized canoe to yet another islet, together with three local women, and we began the crossing.

255

One of the women was extraordinarily beautiful; all three were smiling at me. We exchanged no words; there was no need to speak. The sun was going down. Stilt houses appeared on my left. The scenery was stunning and the silence almost tangible. After crossing, I lay on the shore, overwhelmed. There were no cars on this islet and almost no other signs of modernity. I felt I was glimpsing the islands as they might have appeared centuries ago.

After our six years together, Oceania decided to part with me by offering her true face once again. It was, of course, not the first time I was privileged to see it: I encountered it on some outer islands of Tuvalu, in Ha'apai Group in Tonga, Western Province of the Solomon Islands, in the deep interior of Babeldaob Island of Palau and in many other places. But this time I was leaving and this is what I would carry with me no matter where life would take me.

For six years I had traveled by plane, boat and ferry, canoe, by bicycle and kayak, on foot and by car, truck and bus, all around Oceania. It was one of the greatest journeys one can still take on this planet. And one that helped me to understand better the arrangement of the world, because in a way, Oceania is a microcosm of the problems and issues found everywhere.

After six years of this incredible journey, despite its hardships, I felt that I now belonged to Oceania and that it was my duty to speak on behalf of those I was leaving behind—bringing to the world the plight of the islanders through books, images, and films. I was now intimately familiar with this part of the world through my endless voyages and long nights on the shores, from speaking to thousands of people and witnessing the scars left on exploited land, coral and the sea. For years I observed the joy and pain of the people inhabiting this part of the world, participated in their rituals, dances, ceremonies, funerals or simple moments of rest. As the marvelous atolls and mysterious green islands began slowly disappearing under and behind the wing of my plane, I felt that, while still a wanderer, Oceania more than any other place on earth had given me an intangible home worth fighting for.

Some of many who had an impact on the writing of Oceania

Alson J. Kelen with his family on Ejit Island

FAO Pacific Head - Dr. Vili Fuavao

Great Tongan writer Epeli Hau'ofa

Funafala - Mr. Folavu explaining tides

Joseph Veramu in Samoa

Bikini Atoll Trust Liaison Jack Niedenthal

Nakibae Teuatabo - Climate Change Advisor - Ministry of Environment

Paramount Chief and Senator Mike Kabua

Permanent Secretary of Education Teekoa Ietaake

Nauru President Ludwig Scotty

Senator and former Foreign Minister Tony deBrum

Sir Allan Kemakeza-Minister of Forestry and Natural Resources and former Prime Minister of the Solomon Islands

Sumeo Silu - director of Natl Disaster Management Office

Tongan poet Konai Helu Thaman

Vavao Fetui, Samoan lecturer at Auckland University in NZ

Virisila Buadromo Executive Director of The The Fiji Women's Rights Movement